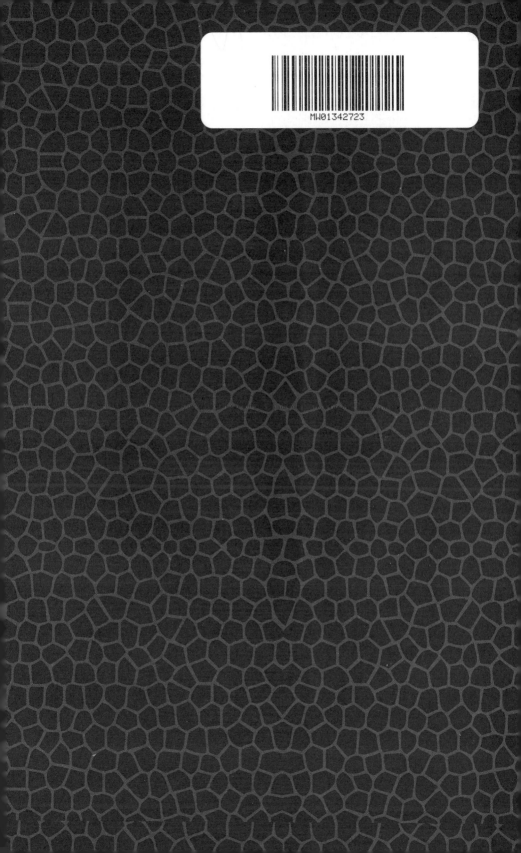

Tranquility
AND Travail

THE MELOHN EDITION

A sequel to Emunah: A Refresher Course
and The Unbroken Chain

Tranquility AND Travail

A Torah Perspective
on the Challenges of Life

RABBI DOVID SAPIRMAN

Copyright © 2021 by Ani Maamin Foundation

info@animaamin.org
845.418.2122
Unauthorized duplication prohibited

ISBN: 978-1-952370-26-7

All rights reserved. No part of this book may be used or reproduced or transmitted in any form or by any means, electronic or mechanical, including photocopying, recording, or by any information storage and retrieval system, without written permission from the publisher.

Published by Mosaica Press, Inc.
www.mosaicapress.com
info@mosaicapress.com

This volume and series is dedicated
in memory of our parents

Joseph and Martha Melohn ע״ה

ר׳ יוסף בן ר׳ אריה לייב הכהן ז״ל
נפטר כ׳ סיון תשמ״ג

ורעיתו מלכה פערל בת ר׳ מאיר ע״ה
נפטרה כט׳ ניסן תשע״ג
תנצב״ה

LEON AND SIMI MELOHN

בס"ד

Rabbi Zev Leff

Rabbi of Moshav Matityahu
Rosh HaYeshiva—Yeshiva Gedola Matityahu

הרב זאב לף

מרא דאתרא מושב מתתיהו
ראש הישיבה—ישיבה גדולה מתתיהו

D.N. Modiin 71917   Tel: 08-976-1138 טל'   Fax: 08-976-5326 פקס'   ד.נ. מודיעין 71917

Dear Friends,

I have read portions of the book "Tranquility and Travail" by Rabbi Dovid Saporman Shlit"a. Rabbi Sapirman presents a comprehensive discussion of the age old question, "Why are there righteous people who suffer and wicked people who prosper". This question was even posed by Moshe Rabbaynu. Ultimately, as the Ksav Sofer explains the answer to Moshe Rabbaynu was, "viraesa achorai upanai lo yareu" – "in retrospect" – when you see the entire plan of existence unfolded – "you will understand" "but looking ahead" – not seeing the whole eternal picture – there is no answer.

However, there are various factors that can make the question easier to deal with, providing options for understanding in general how Hashem's Divine justive functions. Rabbi Sapirman masterfully presents these various factors, weaving them from solid Torah sources, spiced with parables and vignettes to make the ideas more cogent.

I found the work very well organized, lucid, informative and inspiring.

Rabbi Sapirman and his organization "Ani Maamin" have contributed to the Torah world a greatly needed dose of emunah and bitachon. This has been achieved through written and oral shiurim dealing with these topics intellectually and inspirationally.

I recommend this book to every thinking individual, young and old, who wants to strengthen his emunah and bitachon, by appreciating better how Hashem guides and directs the affairs of the world.

I commend Rabbi Sapirman for a quality presentation and pray that Hashem Yisborach bless him and his family with life, health and the wherewithal to continue to merit the community in his many and varied ways.

Sincerely,
With Torah blessings

Zev Leff

Rabbi Zev Leff

שלו' ראובן פיינשטיין	Rabbi Reuven Feinstein
ראש ישיבה	131 Bloomingdale Rd.
ישיבה ד'סטעטן אייללנד	Staten Island NY 10309

ח' כסלו תשפ"א

הנה ידוע לכל דאמונה הוא היסוד הגדול שעליה יכולים לבנות דור ישרים עובדי ה' ואם חלילה יהרס היסוד א"א לבנות כלום. וכמ"ש הגמ' (מכות כד.) בא חבקוק והעמידן על אחת וצדיק באמונתו יחיה. ולדאבונו בזמננו ראינו ירידה נפלאה בעניני אמונה ובפרט בנערינו תשב"ר לומדי הישיבות והבתי ספר. ואם גדיים אין מאין יגדלו תיישים.

וכבר ידוע בשער בת רבים האי גברא רבה ויקירא מזכה את הרבים **הרב דוד ספירמן שליט"א** אשר מסר נפשו והקדיש חייו להשריש אמונה בלבות אחינו בני ישראל. וזכה לסייעתא דשמיא לקרב קרובים ורחוקים ויסד הארגון החשוב **"אני מאמין"** לחזק יסודות האמונה ולהורות להורים ומורים איך ללמד ולמסור לבניהם ותלמידיהם הי"ג עקרים בבירור בלי פקפוקים יתד חזק שלא תמוט.

ועכשיו שלח אלי הגליונות של ספרו **"Tranquility and Travail"** שהוא עומד להוציאו לאור. ספר מלא וגדיש בעניני יסורים וצדיק ורע לו. ואע"פ שאין לי הפנאי לעיין בה כראוי לענין נחוץ כזה נהנתי מאד ממנה ומהמעט שראיתי ניכר שהוא מיוסד על אדני פז של חז"ל שמפיהם אנו חיים מלא חכמה ושכל הישר. והצליח ליתן הגשה נכונה ע"פ תורה להעניינים הקשים האלו דברים העומדים ברומו של עולם באופן צח וברור בהיקף רב ובודאי שכל מבקש שיעיין בו כקטן כגדול ימצא בו חפצו להרחיב דעתו ולתרץ לעצמו ולאחרים הרבה מהשאלות והקושיות הנולדים מהחשך והסתר פנים שאנו חיים בתוכם בסוף הגלות המר הזה.

וע"כ באתי לברכו לראות הצלחה רבה מזה וכל מעשה ידיו להמשיך בעבודת הקדש להטות לבבות ולקרבם לאבינו שבשמים מתוך מנוחת הנפש ובריאות הגוף פרנסה ברווחה ונחת ממשפחתו עד שיסיר המסך ויתיר כל הספיקות בהתגלות מלכותו עלינו לעיני כל חי בביאת הגואל במהרה.

[signature]

Table of Contents

Acknowledgments XI
Introduction 1
CHAPTER ONE: The Mystery. 7
CHAPTER TWO: Tzaddikim and the Good Life 17
CHAPTER THREE: This World and the Next. 23
CHAPTER FOUR: Free Will and the Purpose of Life 42
CHAPTER FIVE: When the Wicked Prosper 55
CHAPTER SIX: Yissurim of the Righteous Are Not for Naught. 63
CHAPTER SEVEN: Yissurim for Atonement 71
CHAPTER EIGHT: Yissurim and Prayer 77
CHAPTER NINE: Great Gifts, but Only through Yissurim 81
CHAPTER TEN: All for the Good 84
CHAPTER ELEVEN: The Mystery of Gehinnom 97
CHAPTER TWELVE: Yissurim and Tzaddikim. 102
CHAPTER THIRTEEN: Responsibility for Others 107
CHAPTER FOURTEEN: A Deeper Glimpse into Divine Providence. .115
CHAPTER FIFTEEN: Gilgul 119
CHAPTER SIXTEEN: Can We Judge? 125

CHAPTER SEVENTEEN: Teshuvah 131
CHAPTER EIGHTEEN: Community versus Individual. 134
CHAPTER NINETEEN: Historical Churban .139
CHAPTER TWENTY: The Churban of European Jewry 167
CHAPTER TWENTY-ONE: Why the Jews? .170

Acknowledgments

This book has been in the making for years. The truth is that no explanations will suffice to remove the mystery of why *tzaddikim* sometimes suffer and why the wicked sometimes prosper. Only the Ribbono Shel Olam knows what His agenda must be for each individual, each nation, and for the world as a whole. However, the Torah has indeed taught us many general principles that can help to reduce the confusion somewhat. It is those general principles that I try to clarify in this volume.

When a person reaches a milestone, the very first thing to do is to express gratitude to the Ribbono Shel Olam for His benevolence. Just as the farmer who brings *bikkurim* and the person who eats a meal thank Hashem—not only for those fruits or for that particular meal but for everything from *Yetzias Mitzrayim* and on—so too must I be grateful to Him not only for this accomplishment but for all the kindness He has bestowed on me throughout my life.

The Ribbono Shel Olam sends many messengers to do His bidding. My gratitude to these *shiluchei d'Rachmana* cannot be sufficiently expressed. Without the support and encouragement of my *eishes chayil*, *shetichyeh*, this book could never have become a reality. May she and I together be *zocheh* (in good health) to see true *Torahdik nachas* from all our children and grandchildren, *b'ezras Hashem*.

Mosaica Press has done an excellent and most professional job of turning a manuscript into a beautifully crafted book. Rabbi Haber and I have been friends for decades, and it is an honor to have been able to share this project with him. Rabbi Doron Kornbluth's insights and comments, as well as his exceptional patience, together with the work of the dedicated staff at Mosaica, have made this project possible.

This book is merely one facet of the ongoing campaign of the Ani Maamin Foundation to strengthen *emunah* in Klal Yisrael. The Ribbono Shel Olam, in His infinite kindness, enabled me to establish the Ani Maamin Foundation over eleven years ago. Its aims include training *mechanchim* in the methodology to present *emunah* issues in a compelling manner and to produce materials, both audio and written, to further this goal. This book is a part of that effort.

Our sincerest thanks to Leon and Simi Melohn for their vision and generosity in making this publication possible. May the Ribbono Shel Olam consider this a great and eternal *zechus* for their entire *mishpachah*.

Without the tireless efforts of Mr. Shlomo Szydlow of Monsey, Ani Maamin would never have even been a dream. His passion, encouragement, and advice were what enabled this organization to become an actual reality. May the *zechus* stand by him always. May he see continued *nachas* from his entire *mishpachah* and always be involved in spreading *kevod Shamayim* in the world!

My utmost thanks to the *Gedolei Yisrael* who have backed and encouraged us with their written *haskamos* and warm encouragement. They include HaRabbanim HaGeonim, *shlita*: Rabbi Shmuel Kamenetsky, Rabbi Aharon Feldman, Rabbi Reuven Feinstein, Rabbi Shlomo Miller, Rabbi Moshe Mordechai Lowy, Rabbi Yaakov Michael Hirschman, Rabbi Elya Brudny, and Rabbi Zev Leff. Harav Avrohom Chaim Levine, zt"l, was most supportive of our efforts.

It is an honor and a pleasure to work together with Rabbi Pinchos Jung, who has lectured around the globe for Ani Maamin. I have learned so much from him and continue to bask in the warmth of his personality through my interactions with him on a daily basis.

Rabbi Moshe Pogrow, our executive director, has injected into our organization a heightened level of passion for our mission, combined with the dedication and know-how to make it happen. May Hashem grant him continued *hatzlachah*.

A special debt of gratitude is due to Rabbi Daniel Mechanic, founder of Project Chazon. I am honored to have him as a friend. He was the pioneer who, long ago, began the campaign to inform the *tzibbur* of the urgent need to substantiate *emunah* to our youth. It is hard to estimate the number of young people he has been *mechazek* over the last few decades. May Hashem grant him the ability to continue his work in being *mezakeh es harabim*.

Rabbi Aryeh Zev Narrow, executive director at the Rabbi Avigdor Miller Legacy Library/Simchas HaChaim Publishing, has been a true and dedicated friend of Ani Maamin since its inception in ways too numerous to list. His efforts in disseminating the works of Rabbi Avigdor Miller, *zt"l*, go hand in hand with the aims and goals of Ani Maamin.

Dr. Jonathan Ostroff has shared many *emunah* insights with me. His expertise in the *sifrei haRishonim* and our longstanding friendship are very meaningful to me.

Rabbi Dovid Engel, *menahel* of the Toronto Cheder, has enthusiastically embraced the work of Ani Maamin and incorporated it into his *cheder*'s curriculum. He has provided me with the opportunity to teach *emunah* subjects to the eighth grade for the last ten years and continues to be a source of constant encouragement and inspiration. May he have continued success in his efforts for *harbatzas haTorah*!

Rabbi Shlomo Noach Mandel has created a shul in Toronto that is most conducive to growth in *ruchniyus*. Our friendship and work together have spanned many decades. May he have ongoing success in his efforts to spread Torah both in Toronto and across Eastern Europe.

Kollel Keser Torah, founded by the Rosh Kollel Rav Avraham Kahn, *shlita*, is a wonderful place to keep the fire of *ahavas haTorah* burning. May the *kollel* continue to grow and serve as a great source of *chizuk* to its participants.

It is hard to find the right words to thank the people who have supported Ani Maamin with financial assistance over the last eleven years. May they have a share in the increased *chizuk* in *emunah* that they helped to bring about.

The encouragement we have received from the many thousands of people who have benefitted from our audio and written *emunah* presentations has given us the strength to persevere in the face of sometimes difficult odds.

Last but not least, I once again thank the Ribbono Shel Olam for allowing me to have some small share in *kiddush Shem Shamayim*, and I offer my fervent *tefillos* to Him to allow me to continue doing so for many long, productive years.

DS
Toronto, Canada
8 Kislev 5780

Introduction

The plain reality of life is that not all we experience is pleasureful. During their lives, most people get plenty of hard knocks. Some have it somewhat easier, others have it harder, but almost every person seems to get their portion of difficulties.

There are people who absolutely refuse to think about the possibility of sickness, poverty, or the inevitability of death. Especially when life is going relatively well, they lull themselves into a pleasant daydream that everything will remain status quo forever. If upsets come along, as they so often do, such people often fall apart. They simply give way to despair, not knowing how to deal with their misfortune.

Hardships are all the more difficult to bear if we have no clear perspective on the purpose of life and the meaning of these travails. How much better it is to have this perspective before any hard times come—and how difficult it is to gain it once we are already in pain. My fervent wish in writing this work, for those who are willing to undertake the pursuit, is to impart a positive perspective on these matters, as taught to us by the Creator Himself in His Torah, while wishing my readers that they should never need to fall back on this perspective.

BEFORE WE START

Before we can even begin, it is necessary to state in no uncertain terms that Hashem does not run the world in the manner in which we think it should be run. He is G-d, and He has an agenda that is, to a great extent, beyond our grasp. The ideas presented here are gleaned from *Tanach* and Chazal, and can offer but a beginning to understanding these mysteries. Nothing we say or do is going to alter the realities of life. Those who have no *emunah* in our Torah see a haphazard world full of inexplicable *tzaros*, and they may be embittered by it. This is nothing new; indeed, it is an ancient problem. Those of us with *emunah* see the same exact world, but we at least have the tools to comprehend that there is a purpose in it all. We know that our Creator once spoke to us at Har Sinai and gave us His Torah. Everything that happens is because He wills it to happen. He can do—and does do—whatever He wants, and everything that happens to each of us is all for the good. He is perfect and beyond our understanding. Therefore, even though we cannot expect to fully understand the agenda of this all-powerful Creator, we are willing to submit to the infinite intelligence of the Ribbono Shel Olam, as transmitted through our *mesorah*.

WHAT WE HOPE TO IMPART

It is our hope to present to the reader numerous concepts that will serve as encouragement and will facilitate the development of increased positivity in our outlook on life. These concepts are the spiritual realities of life as taught to us by our Torah, through Chazal. Here are some of the main issues we hope to clarify:

- The body is merely a garment for the *neshamah*, donned at birth and removed at the time of death. Death is actually the moment of *yetzias neshamah*.
- This world is merely a temporary stopover on our journey to the ultimate destination, the afterlife. It is for that purpose that we were brought to this world in the first place.
- Life in this world is less than a fleeting moment compared to the eternal existence in *Olam Haba* (the World to Come).
- Whatever we undergo in this world has a direct effect on our portion in the afterlife.
- This world is not the world of reward for what we do. That is reserved for *Olam Haba*.

- There are specific reasons why good people sometimes suffer hardships and evil people prosper.
- The Creator's intelligence is infinite, and human intelligence is very limited. Therefore, in all matters that are beyond our understanding, we can rely on His judgment because it is always correct.
- Even the *malachim*, and certainly humans, are not able to discern a consistent pattern in the way Hashem deals with individuals. Although we have been taught some general rules, we don't understand precisely when they apply or when they don't.
- We never pass judgments on what the Creator does. He doesn't need our approval, and it is folly to attempt to judge Him and what He does. A true *maamin* knows that although it can help when we have some understanding of the ways of Divine providence, we fully accept His judgment even when we don't.
- Whatever happens to a person, no matter how unpleasant or painful, is ultimately for a good purpose whether we understand its purpose or not.
- Chazal have taught us many reasons why a person might have to undergo difficulties. We will try to transmit some of their teachings on this subject.
- We never ask for *yissurim*; on the contrary, we ask Hashem not to give them to us. Nevertheless, if they do come (as unwanted as they are), we need to realize that they serve an important purpose. Though not always easy, we should even try to be thankful for them.
- Hashem loves us, whether we are living through a pleasant period or a rough one. *Yissurim are absolutely not an indication of rejection by Hashem.*
- Hashem deals with us as individuals, but also collectively, as a community. Things that are decreed upon a community may affect all the individuals in that community.
- The patterns of history need to be studied if we are to have any understanding of how Hashem runs His world, and more specifically, how He guides His (Jewish) people. These patterns seem to be very consistent.

WHO IS THIS BOOK FOR?

This book is written for readers who are already convinced of *Torah miSinai* and the authenticity of the transmission of *Torah She'baal Peh*. Those who have questions about the Creator, the Torah, or the Oral Tradition are advised to see my first two books, *Emunah: A Refresher Course* (Mosaica Press, 2015) and *The Unbroken Chain: Understanding the Mesorah of the Jewish Oral Tradition* (Mosaica Press, 2019).

In other words, without a clear belief in G-d—and a basic understanding of how He works in the world—it is impossible to really understand why bad things happen to good people. The human perception of what life should be like is not necessarily consistent with the way the Creator has designed it. Only those who know, without a doubt, that the Ribbono Shel Olam Himself has communicated to us, in His Torah, some degree of understanding of life and its occurrences, can internalize the messages presented in this volume. For a person who doesn't possess this belief, or lacks conviction of same, no explanations will make a difference. The true believer knows—even before he starts to contemplate these matters—that the Creator knows what He is doing and that we may question only for the sake of understanding, but never for the purpose of judging.

Some people prefer not to think about the difficulties of life. I believe that attitude is self-defeating, as at some point or another, we all face tragedy and setback. Those who want to be ready for it, and who want to gain an insight into the perspective that the Ribbono Shel Olam has given us, may find some enlightenment in this book. Through understanding His workings, we may grow closer to Him.

EASY TO WRITE, HARD TO FEEL

Rav Sholom Shwadron used to tell a story: When he was young, a child in his courtyard got hurt, and he carried the boy to the doctor. There was an older woman sitting outside who could not see well. She calmly announced that no one should be alarmed, as it was surely nothing serious. However, this child was actually her own grandchild, so Rav Shwadron held the child up closer so she could see who it was. No sooner did she recognize him than she began to scream hysterically,

"Meir'ka, Meir'ka! *Oy vey!* What happened to you?" Rav Shwadron used to say that when it is someone else's Meir'ka, people say not to be alarmed. When it's their own Meir'ka, they scream.

It's precisely the same when it comes to writing about *yissurim*, their benefits, and how everything is ultimately for the good. So easy to say and write. That's only when it is someone else who is hurting. The writer may be sitting at a comfortable desk, perhaps sipping a cup of hot cocoa, but it's not quite so easy for the person undergoing the suffering. No matter what the nature of the *yissurim* may be, the one who is suffering will almost invariably have to struggle to feel that *yissurim* are beneficial and for his own good.

Nevertheless, write we must! At least we will know with our intellect what the Ribbono Shel Olam has taught us about these matters. Then, hopefully, we can endeavor to internalize that information into our emotions.

This manuscript was prepared way before anyone dreamed of the coronavirus. This paragraph, however, is being written in April 2020 after many have succumbed to this disease, and many remain ill, struggling for their lives. Most people are under lockdown, doing their best to prevent themselves and others from catching this disease. The economy has been destroyed, affecting many of us. At a time such as this, we need *chizuk* and understanding of Hashem's *Hashgachah* more than ever.

May Hashem allow this work to bring the reader *chizuk* and tranquility in dealing with the more difficult situations in life, may we all be spared from them.

CHAPTER ONE

The Mystery

The workings of Divine providence appear to be a colossal mystery. The degree of human suffering confounds us, leaving us with no obvious way to understand how the Creator is running the universe. This can be perplexing and quite disturbing, even for someone who is a total believer.

Deep down, we know that there is a Creator Who gave us both the Written and Oral Torah. We trust, without a shadow of a doubt, that everything contained in that Torah is the word of Hashem. Yet, nevertheless, situations often arise that confuse a person with painful doubts about occurrences that are beyond his comprehension. Sometimes these events can even cause people to feel upset with Hakadosh Baruch Hu, whether they say so openly or only harbor these thoughts in the inner recesses of their hearts. The purpose of this volume is to enable the reader to serve the Creator with a greater sense of tranquility and to be at peace with Hakadosh Baruch Hu; to go through life with the understanding that the One above knows precisely what He is doing, even when we do not (and, really, cannot) understand.

MAKE NO MISTAKE

I have no special ability to unravel any mysteries of Divine providence. However, my purpose here is to remove the popular impression that we have no inkling—not even a little bit—into the way Hashem runs

His world. Many of us assume that we can't make any sense out of it whatsoever.

Such thoughts negate our entire *mesorah* AND weaken our *emunah*; they can cause a person to be unnecessarily embittered and rob him of the peace of mind that ought to be the possession of every believing Jew.

These ideas are simply not true, and the aim of this book is to correct this error and share, from our *mesorah*, whatever information we are privy to.

WHAT WE KNOW AND WHAT WE DON'T KNOW

Although we cannot fully see or understand the complete *Hashgachah* pattern in events that seem disturbing, at least some general principles have been revealed to us. Although we don't see, and perhaps *can't* see, a consistent pattern in how these principles are implemented, at least they provide us with partial answers. Some of these concepts are openly expressed in *Tanach*. Others were known to Chazal in a direct *mesorah* from Sinai or from their understanding of the verses in *Tanach*, which convey the *d'var Hashem* to us.

Our task here is not to explain the matters that have not been clarified in the *mesorah*. That is impossible. Rather, our goal here is to point out those ideas that have indeed been told to us explicitly in the *mesorah*, things we are able to understand and are actually not difficult at all. When we shed at least partial light on the system, we can begin to appreciate the *Hashgachah*, the parts we do understand—and the parts we don't.

WHAT IS THE PROBLEM, REALLY?

Which question is it that gnaws away at our conscience and causes us doubts?

With little doubt, it is the classic question of why the righteous sometimes suffer while the wicked sometimes prosper. In other words, why "bad" things happen to "good" people, and vice-versa. In one form or another, this is the central question about G-d's conduct in the world.

Why can't the world be run in the seemingly logical way? According to our thinking, the people who fulfill Hashem's will, His *tzaddikim*, should be showered with all types of benefits; every *tzaddik* ought to be living the good life, and every evil person should be getting his punishment.

Yet we see that it is not so. Sometimes even the best of people are afflicted! Any thinking person is sometimes bothered by at least some of these most basic questions:

- Why do wicked people sometimes live in tranquility and enjoy life?
- Why does Hashem allow so much suffering and discomfort in the world?
- Why is there so much sickness and poverty?
- Why do babies sometimes die? Surely not because of their sins!

Our *emunah* dictates that Hakadosh Baruch Hu is fair, yet sometimes things don't seem so fair to us. This question has been asked again and again, thousands of times over, in the course of generations. Who knows how many people have stopped believing and left the fold because of things that disturbed them about the way that Hashem has dealt with themselves or others, which they consider harsh or unfair?

Especially in our days, after the destruction of European Jewry in the Holocaust, when people are asking, "Where was Hashem?" There is little doubt that numerous Jews lost their faith in G-d due to the Holocaust.

THE SEEMING CONTRADICTION

Perhaps if we define the question a bit better, it will be easier to find a satisfactory answer. A book was published some years ago (which I personally never read, but was told about), which deals with the subject of why bad things happen to good people. The writer is not a believing Jew, and his thesis is that the Creator is not involved in human affairs such as sickness or suffering. After all, how could G-d, our merciful Father, do such things to his children? What caused the writer to come to this conclusion? He had a son who suffered from some kind of degenerative disease and died as a young child. The writer simply couldn't imagine that an *av rachaman*, a merciful father, would allow—or do—such things. Therefore, he came to the conclusion that this world is an unsupervised, haphazard world. Hashem is not in control of those matters, either because He can't be or because He doesn't want to.

A person who doesn't share in the classic monotheistic belief in an all-powerful and all-knowing G-d, and doesn't believe in the Torah, is not restrained from following his imagination to say whatever he wants about the Creator. We could ask the author of that book, "How do you know that Hashem is a merciful Father? After all, you don't believe in the Torah. You never met the Creator, you can't see Him, and you have never spoken to Him. So maybe He is indeed involved in worldly affairs after all, but He is sadistic and cruel. How do you know?" That author has no way of deciding whether Hashem is merciful or not. He simply prefers to believe that He is indeed kind and loving, and he therefore concluded that Hashem is not involved in human affairs.

However, guesswork will tell us nothing about the essence of the Creator because He is beyond our grasp. No human being can independently know anything about Hakadosh Baruch Hu, what He does and how He works. How could we? We are mortals, and He is—G-d. All we know and all we *can* know is whatever Hashem Himself has revealed to us. The Torah tells us all we know about Him.

Now we come to the true essence of the puzzle we are dealing with. We, who do indeed possess information given to us by the Creator, look to the Torah for enlightenment. And the Torah tells us exactly the opposite of what the author above wrote. It tells us that these two things—which to him (and perhaps, initially, to us) seem to be contradictory—are both absolutely true:

- Everything that happens in the world comes directly from Hashem, both what we perceive as bad and what we perceive as good. Hashem is the one Who bestows kindness on whoever has received it, and He is the one Who punishes or brings affliction on anyone that is suffering. It is all Divine providence, whether on an individual or communal level.

- At the very same time, Hashem is indeed an *Av Rachaman*; He is all merciful; He loves us as a father to his children, and everything that He does is for the good.

How do we reconcile these two seemingly incompatible concepts?

HASHEM IS IN CHARGE

The idea of Divine providence—that the Creator is involved in and controls the affairs of the world—is one of the most fundamental principles of Judaism, and it is evident wherever we turn in *Tanach*. In countless places, we find that Hashem is indeed behind all that happens:

- It was He Who brought the great flood in the time of Noach, punished the Egyptians with terrible plagues, and split the waters of the Yam Suf for our ancestors to cross.
- Moshe Rabbeinu told Pharaoh in Hashem's name that the plagues were all brought upon him to demonstrate that Hashem is in total control, so he can see with his own eyes that Hashem runs the world. One example: "I will separate on that day the land of Goshen where my people stay, that there shall not be there any mixture of wild animals, in order that you should know that I am Hashem, right here in the land."[1]
- The miracles that continued throughout the forty-year stay in the desert, including the *mann* that fell from heaven every day to supply a people of millions with food, all demonstrated Hashem's mastery over the world.
- When Korach and his colleagues were swallowed by a miraculous earthquake, there was no doubt but that this was the work of Hashem.
- Whenever the Jewish People stepped out of line during their stay in the desert, there was open Divine retribution.
- The predictions of the *Tochachah* and the song of *Ha'azinu* (which have all been fulfilled) reflect Hashem's total control and involvement in all the affairs of mankind.

---

1   *Shemos* 8:18.

- Throughout history, whenever travails were brought upon people, whether on a nation, a community, or on an individual, they were always attributed by the *Tanach* directly to the Creator.
- It was Hashem who exiled the ten tribes.
- It was He who brought Nevuchadnetzar against the Jewish People and orchestrated all the terrible retributions that took place at that time of the *churban*.
- Finally, it was He Who led us into exile. All these frightful things were foretold in detail in the Torah and by the prophets.

Nothing should have come as a surprise. Nor have any other sufferings and punishments ever happened by themselves. All are attributed to Hakadosh Baruch Hu. This is the principle of absolute Divine providence in all happenings that occur in this world.

A MERCIFUL FATHER

The point is that Hashem is responsible for *everything* that happens. And yet, the second principle, in seeming contradiction to all the above, is that Hashem is there for us, loves us, cares about us, and that *everything* He has done (or is presently doing) is all for our own good.

He considers us His children. Even when He rebukes us, it is with fatherly love. Here are just a few examples:

- "Because of Hashem's love for you, and because of the oath which He swore to your forefathers, He took you out with a strong hand and redeemed you from the hand of Egypt."[2]
- "You are children to Hashem."[3]
- "You should know in your heart that just as a man rebukes his son, so Hashem rebukes you."[4]
- On the last day of his life, Moshe Rabbeinu forewarns the people against turning away from Hashem. He asks the people how they can even consider rebelling against Hashem, Who is their Father and has done so much for them. "Are you going to do this to

---

2 *Devarim* 7:8.
3 *Devarim* 14:1.
4 *Devarim* 8:5.

Hashem? He is your Father, Who possesses you, made you, and established you!"⁵ This was stated by Moshe Rabbeinu at the very end of his life. By that time, the Jewish People had literally been slammed, time and time again, for each of their mistakes during their forty-year sojourn in the desert.
- David HaMelech says in *Tehillim* that Hashem's goodness and mercy extend to every creature: "Hashem is good to all, and His mercy is upon all that He has made."⁶

Hashem is good to all His creatures; He loved our forefathers, and He loves us, their descendants. Why, then, is there so much suffering in the world? Why can't He be a little more forgiving when we slip up? Why must the retribution be so harsh? Why does He punish the *tzaddikim* too? In all the travails and punishments throughout history, not only the wicked died, but many of the righteous died too. How do we make sense of this?

SEEMINGLY HARSH

Even the punishments that came as retribution for identifiable sins, like *churban Yerushalayim* and *galus Yehudah*, still seem very harsh to us. And in each tragedy, many *tzaddikim* died as well as young children and even babies. Yet, the *Tanach* attributes all of these calamities exclusively to Hakadosh Baruch Hu, no matter how excessive they may seem to us.

In a way, the challenge is even greater: The more He loves us, the stricter and more exacting He is with us. The *Navi* tells us that Hakadosh Baruch Hu's love is expressed all the more through the severity of His punishments! He loves us so much that He punishes us for all our sins. The *Navi* says: "Hear the word that Hashem has spoken about all the family that I brought up from the land of Egypt, saying: I love only you from all the families of the earth. Therefore, I visit upon you all your sins."⁷

---

5   *Devarim* 32:6.
6   *Tehillim* 145:9.
7   *Amos* 3:2.

What does that mean? Can we fathom that? It is as if the Creator is declaring, "Since you are my favorite, I punish you for all your sins, and don't let you get away with a thing." Is this how one treats his children?

> ## Summing Up
> By now we've come full circle, and the question that we are dealing with couldn't be clearer—yet at the same time more complex. How can we begin to understand that Hashem is an *Av Rachaman* Who loves us, the trustworthy G-d Who is all fairness, and nevertheless, not only does He not overlook our sins—He punishes with very strict punishments, not only those who are guilty of the sins but also the seemingly innocent?

THE NEGATIVE OUTCOME

The dangers of remaining with this question are significant. One could—consciously or not—conclude that the *tzaddik* gains nothing by being a *tzaddik*. His end is dark and gloomy, he goes through agony in his lifetime, and leaves this world suffering! Of what benefit was his righteousness if he suffered until the last minute of his life and then he died? Such a life seems to be a worthless, wasted failure. After all, he did everything right, and bad things happened to him anyway.

Likewise, when we see a wicked person whose life is going well for him, we can too easily get the feeling that there's nothing to be lost by disobeying the Torah. He does everything wrong and still enjoys life. At surface level, crime pays!

This question is not new. As long ago as the beginning of the Second Beis Hamikdash, Malachi HaNavi heard similar talk from the people of his generation. These people said that they look up to the wicked who prosper and are not punished by Hashem. There is, therefore, no purpose in following the mitzvos because it makes no difference in a person's life.

> *Hashem said, "You have spoken very strong words against Me."*
> *You said [in response], "What did we speak against You?" You*

said, "It is worthless to serve G-d. What do we gain when we keep his charge? We regress because of the Lord of Hosts. Now we glorify the wicked. Those who do wickedness are built up. They have tested Hashem and escaped."[8]

Indeed, this subject is so important that it has been dealt with throughout the ages.

Because misunderstanding this subject can have such a detrimental effect on one's service of G-d—whether one realizes it or not—it is crucial to gain clarity on these issues. Our aim here is to show that the *tzaddik* is ultimately the winner, and the evil man is unquestionably the loser. Delving into this issue follows in the line of great Jews who focused on the same point:

- David HaMelech devoted the entire seventy-third chapter of *Tehillim* to this issue. He describes how people look at the good people who suffer and the wicked people who prosper, and draw all the wrong conclusions.
- Shlomo HaMelech spoke of this as well. One of the often-repeated themes of *Megillas Koheles* is that since retribution does not come right away, there is confusion, which subsequently gives people license to sin. "That the matter of evil is not done quickly, and therefore people's heart are filled to do evil. That the sinner does evil hundreds of times, and length of time is given to him. Also, I know that it will be good for those who fear G-d, those who have fear before Him."[9]
- When Yirmiyahu saw the prosperity and power of Nevuchadnetzar, he asked Hashem why He allows the wicked to be so successful. "You are righteous, Hashem, when I argue with You. But I will debate with You. Why is the path of the wicked successful, and all the treacherous ones are tranquil?"[10] He, too, was puzzled by this. (However, he did preface his words

---

8   *Malachi* 3:13–17.
9   *Koheles* 8:11–12.
10 *Yirmiyahu* 12:1.

by saying that Hashem is righteous before he argued with Him. In other words, he knows Hashem's ways are just, but he just doesn't understand).

I HAVE NO SECRET INFORMATION

It's almost a chutzpah for someone such as myself to approach such an awesome topic, because I have no insider information and no secrets to share. What I have merely tried to do is to gather and organize some of the teachings found in the Torah. I hope to present them in a manner that will make them easily understandable. My aim is to show that we are not entirely groping in the dark, and that there is a doorway to understanding Divine providence. Certainly, we will not fully understand the subject, and we will not be able to explain why one particular *tzaddik* fares better than another and one *rasha* has it worse than another. Nevertheless, at least understanding the general principles will enlighten our response to the things that happen around us, and we can then be at peace with ourselves and with our Creator.

THIS IS THE CLASSIC KASHYA

In essence, this is the classic challenge of history: "The *tzaddik* who suffers and the *rasha* who prospers." We are taught that Hashem loves us, and all that He does is for the good. Yet the happenings of the world seem to be in stark contradiction to this principle. Moshe Rabbeinu asked it of Hashem on Har Sinai. We will return to Hashem's answer later on. In a sense, this is the central question of life.

CHAPTER TWO

Tzaddikim and the Good Life

One would think that *tzaddikim* are the people who most deserve to have a good life. After all, they are the ones whom Hashem loves most. It should follow that He would grant them good health, ample livelihood, and familial bliss.

But history has shown us that such is not always the case. Throughout the generations, there has never been any such pattern. Indeed, if anything, history has shown a very different pattern.

YAAKOV AVINU

Yaakov Avinu is considered the *bechir she'b'Avos*, the "chosen of the forefathers," as the *Ramban* writes: "The likeness of Yaakov Avinu is inscribed on the throne of glory."[1] What greater indication could there be of his greatness and how dearly Hashem loves him?

Yet we find that Yaakov had a difficult life from beginning to end. A brother Eisav, a father-in-law Lavan, the incident with Dina, the flight from Shechem, the loss of his beloved wife Rachel, and the separation from Yosef. He hardly had a moment's peace in his whole life.

---

1   *Ramban*, Bereishis 33:20.

DAVID HAMELECH

There is hardly any *Tanach* figure more beloved by Hashem than David HaMelech was. Each king who came after him was measured up against him. Some of them did what was right in Hashem's eyes, while others did not measure up so well in doing "as did My servant David." For example, concerning one of the kings, the *Tanach* tells us, "He went in all the sins that his father had done before him. His heart was not complete with Hashem, his G-d, as was the heart of his forefather David."[2] In Yaakov Avinu's blessing before his death, he promised royalty to the tribe of Yehudah, but never specified who from that tribe would begin the dynasty of royalty, or even from which of Yehudah's families royalty would come. Of all the great people in that tribe, it was David in particular who was singled out to be granted the throne *for all eternity*. Mashiach will be a descendant of David.

One would assume that a person so precious to his Creator would be showered with all types of worldly benefits and enjoy a tranquil life in this world, in addition to the infinite reward in the afterlife. But no! Nothing of the sort! David had a very tumultuous life. In his youth he was scorned by his family, and after he was told by Shmuel HaNavi that he would become king, he was chased time and time again by Shaul HaMelech, who wanted to kill him. Many opponents arose against him during his reign, he was severely punished for a sin that he committed, and his own son made a rebellion and attempted to kill him in a manner that would have broken most people. In summation, he had a hard life from beginning to end.

CLOSER TO OUR TIME

We don't have to go back that far in history to find *tzaddikim* who have suffered:

- The Bais HaLevi was asked to divorce his first wife because of vicious slander.

---

2   *Melachim I* 15:3.

- The Malbim was harassed by the *Maskilim* throughout his career as a rav, and was banished from Romania as a result of their libelous slander.
- The Alter from Slabodka had a daughter who was engaged to Rav Naftoli Trupp but died sometime before the wedding. He also lost his son R' Moshe, who died at a young age after the family arrived in Eretz Yisrael.
- The Chafetz Chaim lost his son, Avraham.
- Rav Chaim Ozer had an only daughter, who died in her teens.
- Rav Shach lost a daughter.

This list could go on and on. Then, of course, there were the six million, among whom were many *tzaddikim* and *tzidkaniyos*, who suffered untold horrors and ultimately deaths. It is not really necessary to elaborate on this any further, as we are all familiar with this horrific time in history.

HOW DO THE TZADDIKIM LOOK AT THIS?

The more we look into the matter, the more our amazement increases. It is fascinating that *tzaddikim* who were punished most harshly for seemingly minor sins never complained about it at all. Just the contrary, they were *matzdik es ha'din*—they "justified the judgment" that had come upon them.

They said they have no complaints because it's all fair.

Yet to us it seems very unfair.

MOSHE RABBEINU

Perhaps the most famous example concerns none other than Moshe Rabbeinu. He was forbidden to enter Eretz Yisrael because of the incident regarding the waters of Merivah.

> *Moshe and Aharon gathered the people in front of the rock. He said to them, "Listen now, you rebellious people. Will we take water out of this rock for you?" Moshe lifted up his hand and smote the rock with his staff two times. Much water came forth, and the people and their animals drank. Hashem said to Moshe*

and to Aharon, "Because you didn't believe in Me to sanctify Me before the eyes of B'nei Yisrael, therefore you will not bring this community to the land which I have given to them."[3]

What did he do wrong? It is not completely clear in the Torah, but the *mefarshim* give many explanations as to what Moshe Rabbeinu's mistake was, some of which are as follows:

- *Rashi* says he should have spoken to the rock instead of hitting it.
- The *Rambam* says he lost his temper in public.
- The *Ramban* says that instead of saying, "Will *we* bring forth water," he should have said, "Will *Hashem* bring forth water."

Regardless of what his mistake was, we are certain that Moshe Rabbeinu had no evil intentions whatsoever. He meant only for good. Perhaps he did indeed make one of those mistakes, or whatever else it may have been, but couldn't Moshe Rabbeinu have said to Hakadosh Baruch Hu, "Ribbono Shel Olam, is this my reward for being a devoted leader of the Jewish People for forty years? You know, Ribbono Shel Olam, how much I put up with them! How difficult they made my life, how they spoke and complained against me. Sometimes I was ready to duck because I thought they were going to throw stones at me! I endured it all and fasted forty days and forty nights to receive the Torah for them. Everything I did was for them! I have been the *raaya mehemna* (faithful shepherd) of Your Jewish People for forty years. You also know, Ribbono Shel Olam, that I have only one dream in life: to enter Eretz Yisrael."[4] Moshe certainly could have said all this—after all, he only made *one* mistake...

And yet, Hakadosh Baruch Hu said, "Nothing doing. You committed this sin by the waters of Merivah, and you're not going to Eretz Yisrael."

---

3   *Bamidbar* 20:10–12.
4   The Gemara tells us why Moshe Rabbeinu wanted so desperately to enter Eretz Yisrael. "Rabbi Simlai expounded: Why did Moshe Rabbeinu long to enter Eretz Yisrael? Did he need to eat the fruits? Rather, so said Moshe, 'Yisrael has been commanded many mitzvos that can only be fulfilled in Eretz Yisrael. I will enter the land in order that I shall fulfill them all'" (*Sotah* 14a).

To us, this seems quite unfair. The rest of Moshe's generation—who committed more and worse sins than he—were allowed to enter Eretz Yisrael, but not Moshe Rabbeinu. All of this for one "minute" sin that we have difficulty identifying!

NO COMPLAINT

Moshe Rabbeinu, however, did not register the slightest complaint. On the very last day of his life, he made an astounding declaration, justifying his fate:

> *Whatever the Almighty does is perfect, for all His ways are just. He is the faithful, trustworthy G-d. There is never any unfairness. He is righteous and straight.*[5]

So *we* think that Moshe Rabbeinu was cheated and that he should be dying with complaints on his lips. Yet *he* himself tells the world that Hashem is just and fair in everything that He does! This verse is recited by mourners when they bury a relative, to declare that they accept Hashem's judgment. It is called *tziduk ha'din* (justifying Hashem's judgment). To this day, the Jewish People use Moshe Rabbeinu's declaration of *tziduk ha'din* at that most tragic time in their lives.

YOSHIYAHU HAMELECH

In the *kinos* of Tishah B'Av, we mention the *tziduk ha'din* of Yoshiyahu, said with his last breath. Yoshiyahu took over the throne from a father and a grandfather who were among the worst *resha'im* to ever sit on the throne of David. They made a mess of Klal Yisrael, coerced them into worshipping *avodah zarah*, and even brought idols into the Beis Hamikdash.

Yoshiyahu became king as a child and worked vigorously (for thirty-one years!) to correct the corruptions his father and grandfather had instituted. When he was thirty-nine years old, Pharaoh Necho wanted to lead his armies through Eretz Yehudah to do battle with Aram to the

---

5   *Devarim* 32:4.

north.⁶ Yoshiyahu was so convinced that the people had been totally purified from *avodah zarah* that they would surely deserve Hashem's help in defeating Pharaoh, as promised in the Torah. However, this was not the case because there was still much idolatry committed in secret in Eretz Yehudah. Yoshiyahu rejected Pharaoh's request to let them pass undisturbed, made a fatal error in not consulting Yirmiyahu HaNavi, and went out to battle with Pharaoh. His errors caused a removal of Divine protection. The Egyptian archers shot him with three hundred arrows, and he lay on the battlefield, bleeding from his many wounds and about to expire. When Yirmiyahu heard that he had indeed gone out to battle, he rushed out, but came too late. He found Yoshiyahu lying wounded on the battlefield—about to die—and murmuring to himself. Yirmihayu thought that perhaps he was angry and was accepting *avodah zarah* in protest against Hashem. After all, Yoshiyahu could have rightly said, "Ribbono Shel Olam! Thirty-one years I labored for you, day and night, and brought Klal Yisrael back to Your service. Is this what I get in return? Do I deserve this?" So Yirmiyahu leaned over to hear what Yoshiyahu was saying. He heard no complaint, only a declaration of *tziduk ha'din*: "Hashem is righteous, for I have disobeyed His word."⁷

Once again, we might consider it grossly unfair, but the righteous recipient of the harshness declared it righteous and fair.

Summing Up

Not only do *tzaddikim* not live the good life that we would expect them to have, but they declare that all is fair, expressing no complaints. How do we process all this? How are we to understand and integrate it?

---

6   *Taanis* 22a.
7   *Eichah* 1:18.

CHAPTER THREE
This World and the Next

The following chapter needs to be internalized until it literally penetrates our bloodstream and enters the marrow in our bones. It is one of the most important concepts we can ever learn in our entire lives.

Imagine someone who wants to head toward the west but mistakenly takes the road that leads east. He will end up far from his destination, no?

If we don't know where we are headed, we may not arrive there. To what ultimate destination is life supposed to take us, and what direction must we follow in order to arrive there? When we have clarity on this, it will alter the entire meaning of our lives and provide us with proper direction; we will know on what we should focus throughout our stay in this world.

THE FOCUS OF LIFE

In *Pirkei Avos* we are taught that although Hashem has placed us here, *Olam Hazeh* is not our final destination but merely our passageway to the next world. Rabbi Yaakov says, "This world is a corridor in front of the World to Come. Prepare yourself in the corridor, in order that you shall be able to enter the palace."[1]

A corridor, even a well-decorated one, has no primary purpose other than to lead to the inner rooms. This world, our corridor, may be very comfortable and pleasureful. We may partake of, and enjoy, the many wonderful things Hakadosh Baruch Hu has given us: tasty food, a home, the splendor of a sunset, the beauty of a field full of flowers, and all the other good things of this world that are ours for the taking. However, those pleasures are not the purpose of our coming to this world. The true purpose is that we shall traverse the passageway and arrive in *Olam Haba*.

When we neglect to realize this, our whole perspective on life is skewed because we treat this world as the final destination while it is merely a stopover, albeit a crucial one.

RIDE THE TRAIN

Our stay in this world can be likened to a train ride:

- Sometimes the train is streamlined, the tracks are smooth, and the seats are plush and comfortable. There is a coffee shop, and the train is well air-conditioned.
- Other times the ride is uncomfortable, the train is old, the tracks need repairs, the seats are worn, and the air-conditioning is not working properly.

Either way, what really matters is that we reach our destination. Once we arrive, the details of the journey become forgotten, a thing of the past. Imagine a young child traveling with her mother, asking if she will still have the same seat on the train when she grows up. The mother will surely answer, "Dear child. You won't be here when you grow up. We are only staying on this train a short while. When we reach our station, we will get off."

---

[1] *Avos* 4:16.

THE TWINS' DEBATE

In the *sefer Gesher Hachaim*, the great Gaon, Rav Yechiel Michel Tukazinsky, shares a parable with us.[2] Imagine that there are twin brothers inside their mother's womb, anticipating the end of their stay there. One brother believes in life after the womb. This existence is not the end. There is an entire world on the other side. His brother scoffs at him. "What you see is what you get! At the end of the womb, we just fall off and cease to exist." Suddenly, the believing brother makes his exit, and the remaining brother screams out, "Oh! My brother just died!" However, outside there are shouts of "Mazel tov, it's a boy!"

That is precisely what this world is: nothing more than a passageway to *Olam Haba*.

A TEMPORARY STOPOVER

Rabbi Yosef Leib Bloch[3] used to tell a parable. There once was a man who lived in Europe and decided to emigrate to America. In those years, so long ago, one traveled by ship. He heard that the ship to America would stop in four ports before crossing the Atlantic: Italy, France, Spain, and Portugal. Then it would cross the Atlantic and sail to America. He said to himself, "I don't know the language of any of those countries. When the ship docks and people get off to do a little shopping and sightseeing, I won't understand a single word and won't be able to do a thing!" Since he was an industrious fellow, he got himself a tutor and studied a little bit of Italian, French, Spanish, and Portuguese. Indeed, when the ship docked at those ports, he was able to enjoy himself shopping and conversing with the locals. The only thing that he foolishly forgot to learn was the language of his permanent destination, which was English.

In a similar manner, people who don't keep their sights on *Olam Haba*, but rather devote their lives to the mundane pleasures of this world, are focusing on a very temporary stopover, but are ignoring their permanent destination.

---

2   Part 3, p. 5.
3   Rosh Yeshiva, Telshe, Lithuania.

FOREVER IS VERY LONG

Olam Haba is forever. How long is forever? The Chafetz Chaim used to describe it with a parable. He said, "Imagine that the entire globe was filled with wheat kernels from ground level up to the sky, and there is but one bird eating one kernel every hundred days. It staggers the imagination to think how long it will take for the bird to eat up all the kernels. Eternity is even longer than that, for it is never ending."

AN UPSIDE-DOWN WORLD

If someone views life only from a this-worldly perspective, everything will seem topsy-turvy because our existence in this world is not an end unto itself. If you want to make any sense whatsoever out of the world, you must take into account *Olam Haba* because everything that happens here is connected to our ultimate destiny there, in the afterlife. When we have internalized this, the questions that are asked and the seeming contradictions we have presented become explainable and understandable, at least in part. Therefore, before we go back to the direct question of why sometimes the righteous suffer and the wicked prosper, we need to spend some time discussing *Olam Haba*.

RIGHT FROM THE BEGINNING

At the very beginning of the Torah, Hashem revealed to us the purpose of our creation. The animals were created alive without a *neshamah*, they were a *nefesh chayah*, "living being," as "Hashem said, 'Let the waters swarm with a swarming of *living things*, and birds which will fly over the earth across the firmament of the heavens.'"[4]

But Adam, the first man, was naught but a lifeless figurine until he was given a *neshamah*, as it says, "Hashem Elokim formed man with dust from the earth, and He blew into him the *neshamah* of life. [Then] man became a living being."[5] Then, and only then, did Adam become a living entity.

---

4 *Bereishis* 1:20.
5 *Bereishis* 2:7.

The expression "*neshamah* of life" has two meanings:
- The *neshamah* gives physical life, for only as long as the *neshamah* is inside the body can the person continue to live. Death is defined as the moment of *yetzias neshamah*, when the soul leaves the body.
- But the "*neshamah* of life" means much more. The *neshamah* enables us to achieve eternal life in *Olam Haba*, where we will live on forever, even after death. The essence of a human being is his *neshamah*, not his body. The body is merely a cloak, a covering, for the *neshamah*. Since the journey through this physical world is necessary in order to earn that eternal life, the spiritual *neshamah* was provided with a physical body with which to function and do what it has to do in this world. The *Tanach* tells us that the flesh, skin, veins, and bones are merely a covering and a garment, as it says: "With flesh and skin you clothe me, with veins and bones you cover me."[6] If the skin and the flesh are the garment, and the veins and the bones are merely a covering, what is left to be "you?" The real you is the *neshamah*. The body is just a garment for the *neshamah*.

When Hakadosh Baruch Hu first appeared to Moshe Rabbeinu at the burning bush, He told him to take his shoes off: "Take your shoes off from upon your feet, for the place upon which you stand is holy ground."[7]

Besides the literal meaning, Hashem was conveying another idea. Just as the shoe enables us to walk on rough or pebbly ground, so too, the body enables the *neshamah* to travel through this material world. Moshe Rabbeinu was told to disrobe himself from his physical connection to the world in order to enter the spiritual world of prophecy, as symbolized by the taking off of the shoes.

ONLY A JACKET

There was a tragic story that I once heard when I was in Montreal. The grandson of a famous Rosh Yeshiva had been killed in an accident.

---

6   *Iyov* 10:11.
7   *Shemos* 3:5.

At the funeral, the deceased's brother was inconsolable and very distraught. His zeide went over to him and said, "It's only a jacket." In other words, the *neshamah* is still there, the *neshamah* lives on. After hearing this, the boy calmed down.

The famous rabbi and psychiatrist Rabbi Abraham Twersky was present at a meeting of mental health professionals. One of the doctors there asked him, "Dr. Twersky, do you really believe that you have a soul?" Rabbi Twersky answered, "No! I don't *have* a soul, I *am* a soul. I *have* a body."

The essence of a human being is not his body. Rather, the real you is your soul, your *neshamah*. When you look in the mirror and see yourself, that's not the real you. The real you is your soul.

THE LONG JOURNEY DOWN

In Radin, where the Chafetz Chaim lived, there was a boy who was not totally mentally adept. He used to hang around the yeshiva, and the boys would make sport of him. One day, Chatzkele simply disappeared. When he came back the next day, the boys asked him, "Chatzekele, where were you?" He said, "I went to the marketplace in Eisheshok." The boys asked him, "So what did you get there?" Chatzkele said, "I didn't buy anything. All I brought back was a *shmeck tabak* (a bit of sniffing tobacco)." The boys all started laughing and said, "Look how silly Chatzkele is. He went all the way to the marketplace in Eisheshok and came back with nothing more than a little snuff."

The Chafetz Chaim got wind of this and gave a talk in the yeshiva for the *bachurim*. He said, "If Chatzkele went to Eisheshok and came back with nothing more than a *shmeck tabak*, that's not so terribly funny. But if the *neshamah* comes down to this world all the way from the *olam ha'neshamos* (the world of souls) and departs with even less than a *shmeck tabak* because it earned nothing—that's really laughable and silly." The *neshamah* was put here for a relatively short period of time to earn its keep. The profits are earned through the fulfillment of mitzvos and the study of Torah. This is the purpose and the ultimate goal of a person's existence in this world. How foolish to waste the opportunity!

REWARD AND PUNISHMENT

Olam Haba is completely spiritual. *Rambam* states: "In the World to Come there is no body, only the souls of the righteous with no body, like the ministering angels."[8] There is no physical body, no eating or drinking, or other physical activities. It is the place where each individual will receive what he or she earned during his time on this earth. Every deed will be reckoned and paid for, both the good and the not so good. Nothing is forgotten, nothing overlooked. Hakadosh Baruch Hu does not cheat any creature; everyone gets exactly what is coming to him or her. Even a *rasha* who did some mitzvah will receive his reward, and even a *tzaddik* who did some *aveirah* will have to receive his punishment. Since it is justice that Hakadosh Baruch Hu wants, it has to be even on both sides.

The reward that a person receives for mitzvos is not paid in this world, as Chazal say: "There is no reward for a mitzvah in this world."[9] True, a person may sometimes receive fringe benefits in this life for good deeds performed, but that is not the actual reward. The principal remains for *Olam Haba*. The Torah tells us: "Keep the commandments which I command you today to do them."[10] Chazal explain that this means that "today [in this life] is to do them [keep the commandments], but tomorrow [in the afterlife] is the time to receive their reward."[11]

There are some exceptions to these "otherworldly" rules:

- Sometimes a *rasha* will receive his full reward in this world for a mitzvah he once did. The Creator doesn't want him around in the afterlife, but all debts must be paid, so no mitzvah is overlooked. Therefore, Hashem pays him his reward in this world, the account is closed, and the slate is cleaned. When he gets to *Olam Haba*, Hashem will owe him nothing more.

---

8   *Rambam, Teshuvah* 8:2.
9   *Kiddushin* 39b.
10 *Devarim* 7:11.
11 *Eruvin* 22a.

- Sometimes a good person will receive the punishment for his sins in this world in order for him to arrive in *Olam Haba* with a clean slate. We will write extensively about this in a later chapter.

HASHEM KNOWS HOW TO JUDGE

Rambam, after stating that a person has total free will to do right or to do wrong and to do *teshuvah* for his sins or not, tells us that Hakadosh Baruch Hu knows who, when, and how to punish, sometimes in this world, sometimes in the next, and sometimes in both:

> *When a person or the people of a district sin, the sinner does the sin from his own mind and his own will, as we have said. He deserves to be punished, and Hakadosh Baruch Hu knows how to punish. There are sins for which the judgment requires that he should be punished in this world, whether in his body or property…There are sins that are punished in the afterlife, for which the sinner suffers no harm in this world. There are sins for which the sinner is punished both in this world and in the next.*[12]

This is a fundamental part of our classical belief. In another passage, the *Rambam* states that Hashem has His own unique way of measuring merits and demerits:

> *There are merits that are comparable to many sins…and there are sins that are equal to many merits. It is not determined by numbers, one against one, but rather by other criteria known only to Hashem, and no human being is able to fathom it. The measuring [of sins and mitzvos] is done only by the G-d of knowledge, for only He knows how to weigh the merits against the demerits.*[13]

If no one other than Hakadosh Baruch Hu can measure *aveiros* against mitzvos, then even the *malachim* cannot comprehend Hashem's method

---

12   *Rambam, Teshuvah* 6:1.
13   *Rambam, Teshuvah* 3:2.

of weighing the merits and demerits of each individual—and certainly humans can not.

THE ULTIMATE PLEASURE

Chazal say that the enjoyment of the afterlife is infinitely greater than all the pleasures of this world: "One moment of gratification in the afterlife is better than all of this life."[14] Imagine if we were able to combine all of the pleasures that have ever been experienced in this world—all the physical and intellectual pleasures, all of the fun and excitement—into one person, in one moment. Can you imagine the degree of ecstasy? The Rishonim tell us that even that does not compare to one second in *Olam Haba*.

What does the pleasure of *Olam Haba* consist of? It is the pleasure of basking in the radiance of the Shechinah, the Divine Presence. No human can comprehend such infinite pleasure. Even the prophets were never shown *Olam Haba*. The *Navi* writes: "No eye but Yours, Hashem, has seen what will be done to the one who waits for it."[15] Not even the *nevi'im* can perceive the pleasure of *Olam Haba* because the pleasure of *Olam Haba* is the closeness to the Divine presence. Just as we cannot see the Shechinah in this world, as it states, "No man can see Me and live,"[16] so, too, we cannot perceive the greatness of *Olam Haba*.

To sum up this concept, *Olam Haba* is far, far greater than *Olam Hazeh*, beyond our wildest imagination, both in quantity and quality. It lasts forever, and the pleasure is beyond our comprehension.

It isn't surprising that we don't have an appreciation for the afterlife. Imagine someone offering a six-year-old child the choice of one of two gifts. Either he will receive a new bicycle right now or become the CEO of the giver's corporation upon reaching age twenty-five. Undoubtedly, the child will choose the bicycle. He has no appreciation for the other gift, no matter how much more valuable it is than the bike.

While we are in this physical world, we can only perceive physical material things. We have little appreciation for *Olam Haba* because it's

---

14   *Avos* 4:17.
15   *Yeshayah* 64:3.
16   *Shemos* 33:20.

all spiritual, but we have been taught that the ecstasy of *Olam Haba* is infinitely greater than anything we can imagine in this world.

THE NESHAMAH RETURNS TO HASHEM

Shlomo HaMelech says in *Koheles* that when a person's time in this world is up, his soul returns to his Maker. "The dust returns to the earth, as it once was. The spirit will return to Hashem, Who gave it."[17]

After the *neshamah* departs from the body, it must give an account for everything the person did while he was still in this world. As Chazal say: "Akavya ben Mehalalel says, 'Contemplate three things and you will not come to sin…and before Whom you must give a reckoning…before the King of Kings, Hakadosh Baruch Hu.'"[18]

The Sages also said that after the death of the physical body, each person sees a review of his whole life. It will be similar to watching a video, in which a person will be shown *everything* that he did—in his entire life. "At the time that a person departs from this world to his eternal place, all of his deeds are enumerated before him, and he is told, 'Such and such you did in such and such a place on such and such a day.'"[19]

Everyone, in all of history, who has already departed from this world went through such a judgment immediately after death. Then followed the stages of reward and punishment:

- Eternal Gan Eden for those who have merited it.
- A (temporary) stay in Gehinnom for those who sinned in this world and need to be cleansed.

This is what we call *Olam Haba*.

THE JUDGMENT OF GEHINNOM

Standard Divine punishments are not for the purpose of revenge.[20] When a person sins, the *neshamah* becomes soiled and cannot enter the palace of Hashem in such a state. Therefore, Gehinnom was created

---

17   *Koheles* 12:7.
18   *Avos* 3:1.
19   *Taanis* 11a.
20   Rambam, *Teshuvah* 5:5, refers to the punishment of those who lose their entire share in *Olam Haba* as "revenge."

for the purpose of cleansing the *neshamah* so that whenever its allotted time is over, that *neshamah* will be able to enter Gan Eden to receive its reward. Gan Eden is Hakadosh Baruch Hu's palace, so to speak, and there the *neshamah* will bask in the radiance of His proximity.

Chazal say: "The judgment of the wicked of Israel in Gehinnom is twelve months."[21] This is the case for the average person who committed sufficient sins to qualify being called a *rasha*. If someone says Kaddish for the deceased, it lightens their punishment in Gehinnom. It is for this reason that we say Kaddish for only eleven months; we don't want to give the impression that we think the deceased needed the maximum term. Nonetheless, there are worse *resha'im* who remain in Gehinnom for a longer time, and even people who lose their share in *Olam Haba* completely for certain very serious sins. The worst *resha'im*, such as the Hitlers and Hamans, stay much longer—perhaps forever.

WE NEED TO BE PATIENT

Everyone must eventually, after death, give a final accounting of his life. At that time, all accounts will be settled, so to speak.

Imagine a king who invited his servants to a ball, both the higher-ranking ministers and the officials who have lower positions. The ball was divided into two time slots:

- From six till eight in the evening would be the ball for the lower-ranking officers. That would be served in the outer ballroom.
- From eight till ten the bigger (and better!) banquet will be served in the inner ballroom for the more distinguished people.
- Around a quarter to nine, the VIPs begin to arrive, and they have to go through the outer hall to get to the inner hall. They see that the lower-ranking officers are gorging themselves, but there is nothing served for the "higher-ups" yet. As to be expected, they start to complain. The maître d' tells them to just be patient; a much better feast awaits them in the inner ballroom. They just have to wait a little while for it until it's their turn. So, too, must everyone wait for the "tomorrow" when it is time "to receive their reward."

---

21   *Shabbos* 33b.

THE PIOUS PEOPLE OF OTHER NATIONS

Even good people who are not Jewish can get a share in the World to Come, as *Rambam* says: "The pious of the nations of the world can also have a share in *Olam Haba*."[22] It is most noteworthy that such a statement has rarely been made by other religions, *l'havdil*. They are generally not willing to grant anyone of a different faith the slightest share in Paradise. They maintain that everyone else but they is damned eternally for not accepting their god or their prophet. But in our Torah, it says that *chassidei umos ha'olam*, "the good ones of the nations of the world," can have a share in *Olam Haba*. Of course, if you pay only seven dollars for your ticket, you won't get the same seat as if you paid six hundred and thirteen dollars. The nations that have only *sheva mitzvos B'nei Noach* will get a back seat, while a Yisrael will get a front seat. If they want to get a front seat, they will have to join us by becoming *geirim*. Nevertheless, the pious of the other nations can have a share in *Olam Haba*.

RETIREMENT

After death, there are no more opportunities to earn reward. The time of profit making is only while a person is alive in this world. One reaps the harvest he sowed in his lifetime but cannot earn additional reward afterward. The period after death is similar to retirement. When people retire from work, they have no new income. They live off whatever money they put away during their working years, or whatever investments they made in their years of employment.

Shlomo HaMelech tells us in *Koheles* that we should do all we can in this life because our opportunities are over after death: "Whatever your hand finds the ability to do, do it with all your might. There are no deeds or calculations or knowledge or wisdom in the grave to which you go."[23]

Ramchal explains each phrase of this verse.

> *A person who didn't do a lot of good deeds in this world cannot do them afterward. Likewise, someone who did not take an*

---

22 *Sanhedrin* 105a; *Rambam, Teshuvah* 3:5.
23 *Koheles* 9:10.

account of himself to see where he stands in life cannot do it afterward. An individual who did not amass knowledge cannot do it afterward. That is what it means, "There are no deeds or calculations or knowledge or wisdom in the grave to which you go." The message is clear. "Don't waste any time in this world, because after you leave it's too late."[24]

When the Vilna Gaon was about to die, his *talmidim* came to see him and discovered that he was crying. They said to him, "*Rebbi*, do you have to cry? You know what a glorious future awaits you in *Olam Haba!*" The Gaon fondled his tzitzis and said, "In this world, for a few coins you buy tzitzis, put them on, and Hakadosh Baruch Hu gives you reward forever for the mitzvah you have done. Those opportunities are over once a person leaves."

Chazal saw the following story in Heaven with their *ruach ha'kodesh*: Reish Lakish, one of the great sages of the Talmud, had originally been the head of a band of robbers. Rav Yochanan guided him to do *teshuvah* and turned him into one of the greatest *chachamim*. On the day that Reish Lakish died, his old buddies from the band of robbers also died. When they got "upstairs," they saw Reish Lakish in Gan Eden, while they were assigned to Gehinnom. They said, "Where's the fairness? We robbed together; we did everything together!" The robbers were told, "He did *teshuvah*, he repented, and you did not." They said, "That's all? So we'll do *teshuvah* too!" The Heavenly response: "No! Now it's too late." The opportunities for *teshuvah* are only available for a person up until the moment of death. After death, the opportunities are over.

DIVIDENDS AFTER DEATH

Sometimes it is possible for a person to receive reward in *Olam Haba* without new accomplishments because one's children can be a merit for him. Their good deeds are a credit to the father. "A son can give *zechus* to a parent [but a parent cannot give merit to a son]."[25]

---

24 *Mesilas Yesharim* 4.
25 *Sanhedrin* 104a.

Chazal say that "a child is the leg of the father," which is usually understood to mean that the son takes after the father. But it has a much deeper meaning as well. In this world we are called *holchim*, those who go—we are on the go and can move, which means that we can accomplish. In the afterlife, even the angels are called *omdim* because they are stationary. They cannot move spiritually higher because they have no free will. When Yehoshua Kohen Gadol (at the beginning of the Second Beis Hamikdash) had a revelation from an angel, he was told that if he would accomplish great things, the merit would enable him to keep moving in the world of stationary beings: "So said the Lord of Hosts, 'If you will go in My ways, keep My mission, and you will also judge My house and guard My courtyards, then I will give you the ability to walk between these stationary ones."

Hence, "the son is the leg of the father" means that the father can move up in the afterlife through the merits that the son, grandchildren, and future generations do for him. A person who started something good in his life can also gain accrued dividends after death from the ripple effect of what he did in his lifetime. Someone who was a *mezakeh es ha'rabim*, taught others Torah, or guided someone to go in the path of Torah, gains credit continually. After all, their descendants carry on, teaching others and teaching their children. If someone healed a sick person, saved a life, or enabled a person to support his family, the merit continues to grow. The one who set these good things in motion gets a share in everything that results from his deed. Such a person can move higher based on the investment he made when he was still in this world.

The Chafetz Chaim, after his death, often appeared in a dream to his daughter, Rebbetzin Zaks. After he had been appearing in her dreams for a while, she said, "Abba, I can't see you so clearly anymore." The Chafetz Chaim said, "From the mitzvos I did in my life, I keep accumulating dividends, so I keep moving higher and higher. Now I'm further away from earth, and therefore it's harder for you to see me."

THE LEVEL OF REWARD

The judgment one undergoes after death is not merely to decide if the gates of Gan Eden will be opened for him or not; it's also to decide *where* one's place will be in Gan Eden. No two portions are alike, and the judgment is to decide not only whether one will get in, but where he will sit and what the degree of his reward will be.[26]

NOT THE END

What happens in this world is not the end of the *tzaddik* at all. Since the place of reward for mitzvos is not this world, that means that, in a sense, death is just the beginning of the *tzaddik*'s existence. How could the reward for a mitzvah be paid in this world? All the enjoyments and pleasures of the whole world together wouldn't be enough to pay for a single mitzvah. It's like trying to buy a bottle of soda and asking the clerk to cash a check for a million dollars. He just doesn't have the change. You just can't buy a bottle of soda with a check for a million dollars. The "check" of a mitzvah is simply too great to be cashed in this world. Therefore, if a person is a *tzaddik* and he goes through difficulties in this life, for reasons we have not yet identified, we cannot ask, "Is this the Torah and this its reward?" No!

This is not the reward of the *tzaddik* at all. A *tzaddik* will enjoy his reward forever, and everything will be paid to him at the time of payment. If the person left this world as a decent person, then his life was a success story. He got to the destination, even if the ride was bumpy. The portion of any righteous person who suffered in this world is not diminished one iota in the eternal world. Not only that; they are even recompensed for the struggles they endured in this world. There the *tzaddikim* are sitting in the front rows, all of their travails long

---

[26] There will be another period of afterlife, known as *techiyas ha'meisim*, the resurrection of the dead, for those who will deserve it. This will occur at the time Hakadosh Baruch Hu will choose. Belief in the resurrection of the dead is the last of the thirteen principles of faith enumerated by *Rambam*: "I believe with perfect faith that there will be a resurrection of the dead at whatever time will be the will of the Creator, may His name be blessed and exalted forever and ever" (*Ani Maamin*, thirteenth principle). At that time, the *neshamah* will be reunited (to some extent) with the body, although it will not be a physical body as we have now.

The era of Mashiach is not related to the subject of the afterlife, because the era of Mashiach is to be a phenomenon of this world, not of *Olam Haba*: "Shmuel said, "There will be no difference between this world and the days of Mashiach except for the servitude of nations, as it says, 'There will not cease to be poor people in the land'" (*Berachos* 34b)."

forgotten, and they will enjoy themselves—forever, in complete ecstasy without end.

Likewise, the end of the wicked man's story is not in this world. All scores will be settled, and nobody will ever gain from doing the wrong thing.

DON'T GRIEVE EXCESSIVELY

We have been commanded not to grieve excessively over a deceased person. As an expression of grief when a relative died, the Emori people used to cut themselves and make a bald spot by pulling out some hair. The Torah forbids us to conduct ourselves this way when a loved one dies, as it says: "You are children to Hashem your G-d. Do not cut yourselves or make a bald spot between your eyes over a deceased."[27] *Ramban* explains, in the name of *Ibn Ezra*, that since we are "children to Hashem," we should trust His judgment in the same way that children trust their parents. Children have an intrinsic belief that their parents have their best interests at heart, even when they don't understand their motives. Therefore, even when a person passes on at a young age, Hashem commands us not to display too much grief because we should believe in and trust Hakadosh Baruch Hu. "Hashem loves you more than a father loves his son. Do not cut yourselves over whatever He does, for all that He does is for the good, even if you don't understand it. Just as little children do not understand what their father does, but still they rely on him." The verse that follows says, "because you are a holy people to Hashem."[28] *Ramban* interprets this as referring to "a promise that the soul continues to live on before Him, may He be blessed. Since you are the holy people and the favorite of Hashem...it is not proper for you to cut or bald yourself over a deceased, even if he died young." Since the holy people are destined for *Olam Haba*, they therefore realize that death is not the end, but only a beginning. The point is that whatever happens in this world is minuscule compared to what awaits us in *Olam Haba*.

---

27 *Devarim* 14:1.
28 *Devarim* 14:2.

WHAT AWAITS THE TZADDIK?

As previously mentioned, Moshe Rabbeinu was forbidden to enter Eretz Yisrael, although he longed to do so. Although it might seem to us that he would have been justified in complaining, nevertheless he declared that Hakadosh Baruch Hu is totally righteous and that there is never any unfairness. When Moshe Rabbeinu davened to Hakadosh Baruch Hu and begged and pleaded to be allowed to go into Eretz Yisrael, Hashem said: "I cannot fulfill that request. I will show you Eretz Yisrael, but I am not taking you in." But Hashem consoled him by saying that although He had His reasons for not granting Moshe's this-worldly request, immense reward awaits him: "There is so much more than this waiting for you, much good hidden away for you [in *Olam Haba*]."[29]

The point is that we have to trust that Hakadosh Baruch Hu knows what He's doing, just as a child trusts a father.

HOW FORTUNATE, RABBI AKIVA

Rabbi Akiva went through a horrible death at the hands of the Romans. They scraped his flesh with iron combs, but Rabbi Akiva was reciting *Shema*, and his soul departed at the word *"echad."* A Heavenly voice came forth and told him how fortunate he was, and he entered *Olam Haba* immediately, with no waiting period.

> *When they took out Rabbi Akiva to be murdered, it was the time for reciting the Shema. They were scraping his flesh with iron combs while he was accepting upon himself the yoke of the kingdom of Heaven. His students said to him, "Our master! Even now?" He said to them, "All my life I was concerned about this verse, 'With all your life,' [which means] even if He takes your soul. I said, 'When will it come to my hand to fulfill it?' Now that it has finally come to my hand, shall I not fulfill it?" He was drawing out the word echad until his soul left him.*

---

29   *Rashi, Devarim* 3:26.

> *A Heavenly voice came out and said, "How fortunate you are, Rabbi Akiva, that your soul left you by the word echad."*[1]

Note that even when undergoing horrible torture, the Heavenly voice was saying, "How fortunate you are."

SUMMING UP THUS FAR

This world is but a fleeting moment compared to the eternity of *Olam Haba*. All the pleasures of this world are nothing in comparison to the ecstasy in the world of *neshamos* that awaits those who deserve it, and all the sufferings of this world are nothing in comparison to the *yissurei ha'nefesh* in the world of *neshamos*.

A person must realize that this world is only temporary, like traveling on a train. Some people seem to have a smooth ride, while others seem to have a bumpy one. But the main thing is to arrive at the destination.

NOW WE CAN BEGIN

Now that we know that this world is merely a preparation for *Olam Haba*, we can go back to the subject we began with. Why do truly righteous people sometimes suffer and truly wicked people sometimes prosper?

The answer is that what happens to people in this world affects their standing in the eternal life. When a person leaves this world, it is not the end of his existence but merely the beginning. The *tzaddik* who suffered will not lose out, and the *rasha* will not gain from his prosperity. With this basic background firmly in place, it is possible to begin to look for more detailed reasons as to why the Ribbono Shel Olam runs the world in this way. We have opened a doorway to begin understanding.

Summing Up

- This world is merely a passageway to the next. It is a very temporary existence, likened to the shadow of

---

[1] *Berachos* 61b.

a bird flying overhead—which lasts only a fleeting moment—in contrast to *Olam Haba*, which is eternal.
- Whatever happens to us in this world will somehow affect our situation in the afterlife.
- This world is not the place to receive reward. Sometimes we may receive fringe benefits here, but the true reward is reserved for *Olam Haba*.
- Whatever occurs to us in *Olam Hazeh* is relatively insignificant.

CHAPTER
FOUR

Free Will and the Purpose of Life

If we are to utilize our lives in this world productively, we need to know why we were put here in the first place and what we are supposed to accomplish during our stay.

The following is a beautiful insight from the *Sefer Hachinuch*:

> *Know, my son, that the only thing that Hashem derives from people doing His mitzvos is that He wants to do good for us. When a person is prepared and ready through doing the mitzvos to receive the good, then Hashem will grant him that good. Therefore, He informed them of the good path [the way of the Torah] so that they can become good people…A special parashah has been written in the Torah to inform us of this fundamental idea. That is what is written: "Now, Yisrael, what does Hashem want from you, etc.,* **only for your good.***" This means that Hashem asks nothing of you in your doing His mitzvos other than that He wants, in His great goodness, to do good to you. As is written after this: "Behold! Hashem, your G-d owns the heavens and the heavens above the heavens, the earth and all that is in it. Only in your forefathers did Hashem delight to love them. He chose their descendants after them*

[that is you], like this very day." This means that He does not need your mitzvos, but only out of His love for you, to give you merit.[1]

The *Ramchal*, in his classic *sefer Mesilas Yesharim*, teaches the same concept:

> Behold! [This is] what the Sages, of blessed memory, have told us, that a person was created only to derive enjoyment from Hashem, and to take pleasure from the radiance of His Shechinah. This is the true enjoyment and the greatest pleasure of all the pleasures that can be found. The place of this pleasure is truly in the World to Come, for it has been created with the preparation needed for this thing. However, the road to reach this destination of our desire is [through] this world. This is what the Sages, of blessed memory, have said: "This world is a corridor in front of the World to Come."
>
> The mediums that can bring a person to this end are the commandments that Hashem has commanded us. The place of doing these mitzvos is only in this world. Therefore, a person has been placed in this world first, in order that, through these mediums available to him here, he will be able to reach the place that has been prepared for him, which is the World to Come, there to be satiated with the good that he has acquired for himself through these mediums. That is what they [the Sages] of blessed memory said: "Today is to do them, and tomorrow is to receive their reward."[2]

BREAD OF EMBARRASSMENT

The *neshamah* entered your body from the *olam ha'neshamos*, where it was basking in the radiance of the Shechinah and was in a state of

---

1   *Sefer Hachinuch*, mitzvah 95.
2   Chap. 1.

tremendous ecstasy. What was the purpose of taking it from there and putting it into this world?

Our *sefarim* tell us that the *neshamah* comes down to this world because of a concept called *nahama d'kisufa*, "bread of embarrassment." This means that if someone is treated to a handout, as much as it may be pleasurable, it is nevertheless embarrassing. It is human nature to want to feel that one has earned and owns what one has, not received it as a handout. We come to this world in order to earn our share in *Olam Haba*. Although the *neshamah* was already there, there was something missing because it was *nahama d'kisufa* and had not been earned. Therefore, the *neshamah* is sent down to this world to be given an opportunity to earn its keep in *Olam Haba*.

The Chafetz Chaim explains this with a parable. There once was a factory that the owner visited only periodically. The daily running of the factory was entrusted to a manager. When the owner would visit, all the workers would line up, and each one would state what his job was and how much he gets paid. When the owner reached the worker at the end of the line, the worker's face turned red and he said, "I am the manager's brother-in-law." In other words, "I don't do anything, but he gives me a salary because I'm his brother-in-law." How terribly embarrassing! That is how the *neshamah* feels in *Olam Haba* before it earns its keep, and therefore Hakadosh Baruch Hu gives us the opportunity to come here and earn our reward. That is the purpose of our coming to this world.

We have now learned that Hakadosh Baruch Hu wants nothing more than to bestow His infinite goodness upon us, to give us the utmost pleasure. However, the Creator's wisdom has decreed that in order for us to receive this ecstasy, we need to earn it. If we were to receive it for free, it would be "bread of embarrassment."

HOW, NOT WHY

It is not in our best interest to question deeply into *why* Hashem runs the world the way He does. It is far too complex for our limited intellect and will only serve to frustrate and disappoint us. What we do need to do, however, is to understand *how* Hashem operates—the rules and regulations of His *hashgachah*—as revealed to us in our Torah.

The sooner we realize that fathoming Hashem's secrets is beyond us, the better off we will be. "Why?" is an irrelevant question. Someone may question why grass is green instead of another color, or why elephants have tusks and lions do not. Just as it is irrelevant to question nature because Hashem knows how to make His world, so too are the "why" questions on what Hashem does. When, occasionally, we have an inkling of an answer, it satisfies our curiosity, and perhaps we feel somewhat enlightened. But when we don't, there is no great loss because we don't need to decide whether we think Hakadosh Baruch Hu is justified in all that He does. What we do need to know is how we are expected to conduct ourselves in accordance with His will. Hakadosh Baruch Hu is always right, even when we have no idea why. We trust Hakadosh Baruch Hu because He knows infinitely more than we do and runs the world the way it needs to be run. When we are able to understand, that is great. However, it's also perfectly okay when we cannot, which, as mere mortals, inevitably happens quite often!

HASHEM'S AGENDA FOR EACH INDIVIDUAL

The Ribbono Shel Olam sets out a game plan for each person right from the start. Before each person comes to the world, there is already a program set out for him. This involves the parameters of his existence and the tests he will need to overcome. No two agendas are alike. As the Gemara tells us, it is decided at the time of conception whether a particular newborn will be strong or weak, wise or foolish, rich or poor. These predetermined circumstances are the parameters of the person's life, the situations and difficulties that he must overcome in order to serve his Creator. The *malach* does not ask if he will be a *rasha* or a *tzaddik* because that is left up to the individual's free will. The choices he makes to deal with his circumstances will determine how much reward he will ultimately receive. This is the basic agenda of the person's life.

> *As Rabbi Chanina bar Papa expounded: "The angel in charge of conception is called Lilla. He takes the soon-to-be-born before Hashem and asks what will be the destiny of this individual. Will he be strong or weak? Wise or foolish? Rich or poor? But*

wicked or righteous he doesn't say, as Rabbi Chanina said, 'Everything is in the hands of Heaven except for the fear of Heaven.'"[3]

The abovementioned parameters are merely the starting point. Free will choices then affect how Hashem deals with the individual:

- He might commit a sin that will cause him a punishment that was not included in the original agenda. This would never have happened had he not slipped up.
- He might do some great deed that will cause Heavenly blessings to be showered upon him that were not originally ordained for him.

One point is clear: the difficulties in a person's life are not necessarily a response to something he has done wrong. They may simply be part of the preordained agenda.

For example, if it had been decreed that a person will be poor, then all the difficulties that come along with poverty are preordained. The distress and embarrassment of scrounging around to pay his bills and to put bread on the table for his family, of being looked down upon as lazy, and of his wife harassing him for not bringing home sufficient *parnassah* are all part of the *nisayon*. All this travail was destined for him as part of his individual agenda and is one of the tests which he will need to overcome. Poverty can be a great *nisayon*. A person who is desperate may be tempted to steal, or he may allow himself to become embittered against Hashem for his lot. He may use his poverty as an excuse to be negligent in the fulfillment of various mitzvah obligations. Alternatively, the person may utilize the desperation of poverty as an opportunity to become humbled and to draw closer to His Creator in prayer.

On the other hand, if it was decreed at the time of conception that the person would be rich, he might live under tremendous pressure. Wealth is certainly not a guarantee of tranquility and can actually cause great distress: "The more property one has, the more worry."[4] He may

---

3   *Niddah* 16b.
4   *Avos* 2:7.

not be able to sleep due to anxiety over a business deal, a threatened bankruptcy, or just because of his extensive business interests. He may be harassed by charity seekers. Wealth can be as great a test as poverty. The Torah says clearly that through riches a person can come to forget Hashem altogether and come to think that he's a self-made man. He may become greedy and overwhelmed from the pursuit of money. His wealth may make him arrogant and self-centered, and he might not give *tzedakah* in proportion to his wealth. Wealth can also be an opportunity for growth. It gives one the opportunity to disburse large amounts of charity, to run a household with an open-door policy for guests, and to feel tremendous gratitude to Hashem for the blessings He has benevolently bestowed upon him.

The extent to which a person's free will choices improve or worsen his lot is entirely up to the Creator and is beyond our ability to fathom. This is what we learn in *Mesilas Yesharim*:

> We find that a person is truly placed in the midst of a strong war. All matters of this world, whether good or bad, are tests for a person. Poverty from one side, and riches from one side. As Shlomo HaMelech said, "Lest I be full and deny, and say, 'Who is Hashem?' or lest I become poor and I steal."[5] Tranquility from one side and travail from one side, until the point that the war is upon him from front and back. If he will be the mighty warrior and be victorious in the war from all sides, then he will be the perfect person who will merit to cling to his Creator. He will exit the corridor and enter the palace to bask in the light of life.[6]

The tests that we undergo are part of the purpose of our coming to this world. As *Ramchal* states: "We have now learned that a person's main existence in this world is to fulfill mitzvos, serve [Hashem], and withstand tests."

---

5   *Mishlei* 30:9.
6   Chap. 1.

FREE WILL

In order for us to earn a place in the afterlife, it is essential for us to have free will. Were there no free will, there could be no justification for either reward or punishment. Free will means that we can choose between good and evil:

- If we make the right choices, we will be deserving of the ultimate reward.
- If we make the wrong choices, we will have to suffer the consequences.

Hashem does not control us or coerce us in either direction. We have total freedom to choose between good and evil, but no control over our circumstances, resources, or abilities. Those are totally in the hands of the Creator: "Everything is in the hands of Heaven except for the fear of Heaven."[7]

The only thing that G-d leaves totally up to us is our ability to choose right over wrong or vice versa—"the fear of Heaven."

HIDDEN HASHGACHAH

If Hashem's agenda for the world requires the existence of free will, then it is obvious that the world cannot run on a system in which the righteous consistently prosper and the wicked consistently suffer. If that were the case, how would it be possible for anyone to choose anything but what is good and righteous, for fear of retribution? If everyone who smoked on Shabbos was struck by a bolt of lightning, then keeping Shabbos would be no test at all. If every *tzaddik* who spends his days in the *beis midrash*, learns Torah with his children, and sends them to yeshiva would also live in a palace and drive a Lexus, there would be basically no opportunity for choice!

In order to earn our reward, we need to be tested regularly with various *nisyonos* throughout our lifetime. These tests vary from one person to the next, and even from one minute to the next.

---

7   *Berachos* 33b.

- One may have a temptation to succumb to lust or cruelty.
- One may be tempted to simply take the easy way out rather than exert themselves sufficiently to do a mitzvah.
- Controlling one's *middos* is a constant challenge. It is easy to be arrogant or respond to vexing situations with anger, while jealousy can destroy a person.
- A person may undergo the *nisayon* of encountering difficulties or being plagued with misfortune of one kind or another. Will he accept his struggles and his pain without complaint? Will he continue to serve the Creator with all his energy? Will his suffering humble him and cause him to realize his own frailty and the futility of this-worldly endeavors? Will it make him grow stronger in his dedication to Hashem's service?

Passing any of these tests is a tremendous *zechus* and a ticket to great reward in the afterlife.

As stated, *nisyonos* are a primary component of our purpose here in this life. *Rashi* tells us that *tzaddikim* should not expect to live in tranquility in this world. Difficulties are part and parcel of our existence and can be put into perspective once one has internalized the purpose of life: "Yaakov wanted to live in tranquility, so the travail of Yosef came suddenly upon him. The righteous want to live in tranquility? Hakadosh Baruch Hu says, 'Is what awaits the *tzaddikim* in *Olam Haba* not enough for them, that they want to live in tranquility in this world as well?'"[8]

Therefore, the world is not run precisely as we would expect—nor as we might like it to be. We are not going to see every good person enjoy an abundance of good and receive his reward immediately, or every bad person suffer in proportion to his wickedness and receive his punishment immediately.

Obviously, this is only a general explanation as to why the pattern of Divine providence must breed confusion. It does not offer any clarification of consistency as to *which tzaddik* will be afflicted and which one

---

8 *Bereishis* 37:2.

will not. Nor does it explain why one particular wicked man prospers and another does not.

We really cannot understand such things. When Rav Aharon Leib Shteinman came to Toronto, he delivered a most inspiring talk. He stated, based on a Gemara, that even the *malachim* do not understand the system by which Hashem deals with individuals in this world!

The point is that we don't—and really, can't—know why some suffer and some do not. Only Hakadosh Baruch Hu knows. We can only give some general rules, but we don't know when He chooses to use each rule. We can say that a *rasha* gets paid in this world for his mitzvos, but we certainly do find *resha'im* who suffer here in this world. We can also find *tzaddikim* who live very prosperous, happy lives. We do not know how to explain this with any consistency, and the pattern is not obvious to us at all.

WHEN WE REALIZE WITH WHOM WE ARE DEALING

Interestingly, after the first verse of *Mizmor Shir L'Yom HaShabbos*, there is not another word in that entire chapter about Shabbos.

> *A psalm, a song for the day of the Shabbos...For you make me happy with Your works, with the deeds of Your hands I rejoice. How great are Your works, Hashem! How deep are Your thoughts. A boor cannot know [this], and the fool does not understand this. When the wicked bloom like grass and all the doers of evil blossom, it is to destroy them till eternity...The righteous man will flourish like a date palm and grow tall like a cedar in Lebanon...To declare that Hashem is just, [He is] my Rock in Whom there is no unfairness.*[9]

Radak explains that the thoughts expressed here are the things we should think about on Shabbos. All week long, people are busy with their work, but on Shabbos they have more time to contemplate these ideas. There are two main themes discussed in this psalm:

---

9   Tehillim 92.

- The wondrousness of G-d's world and how beautiful and inspiring it is.
- The fool does not comprehend that when the wicked prosper, it is for the sake of ultimately destroying them, but that the righteous will ultimately be successful and blossom.

When you think about it, it is not at all surprising that we should connect the wonders of the natural world to the theme of Shabbos. After all, Shabbos is a reminder of the six days of Creation, culminating in the first Shabbos. Therefore, we use the Shabbos day to contemplate that Hashem created the entire universe. But how is the eventual downfall of the wicked and the ultimate success of the *tzaddikim* connected to Shabbos?

In fact, the connection between the two subjects is very simple. When Hashem created the world, He not only made the rules of nature, but He put in place His system of running the world as well. These rules were made to coincide with the Creator's agenda for the world, and are part of the original plan of *maaseh Bereishis*. When we contemplate the infinite intelligence and perfection manifested in the natural world, we begin to realize how puny our minds are in comparison to the infinite intellect of the Creator. We come to see that just as He knows how to set a universe into motion, so, too, does He know how to run it. So, when the fool sees "the wicked sprouting forth like grass and all the evildoers blossoming," he judges the matter with his limited mortal intellect. He doesn't see that the end will be "to destroy them forever." Nor does he perceive the glorious end of the *tzaddik*, who will grow "as fruitful as the date tree and as tall as the cedar in the Levanon forest." When there are things that we don't understand, it is often because our limited human minds *cannot* understand them—we are not tuned in to the Divine plan in the world.

All the above is merely a general idea. Our faith tells us that the details and the consistency are also exact to a hairsbreadth, but here we are limited in how much we are capable of understanding.

PREDETERMINED VERSUS FREE WILL

Everything that happens in the world is controlled by Hashem, but His responses will depend on the choices we make with our free will. Seemingly, then, nothing that happens should be preordained since the outcome will depend on those free will choices.

However, there are a number of verses in *Megillas Eichah* that state that all happenings, whether good or bad, come directly from Hashem.[10] *Rashi* in *Eichah* quotes Chazal:

כִּי לֹא עִנָּה מִלִּבּוֹ וַיַּגֶּה בְּנֵי אִישׁ: לְדַכֵּא תַּחַת רַגְלָיו כֹּל אֲסִירֵי אָרֶץ: לְהַטּוֹת מִשְׁפַּט גֶּבֶר נֶגֶד פְּנֵי עֶלְיוֹן: לְעַוֵּת אָדָם בְּרִיבוֹ ד' לֹא רָאָה: מִי זֶה אָמַר וַתֶּהִי ד' לֹא צִוָּה: מִפִּי עֶלְיוֹן לֹא תֵצֵא הָרָעוֹת וְהַטּוֹב: מַה יִּתְאוֹנֵן אָדָם חָי גֶּבֶר עַל חֲטָאָיו:

> *It is not His desire to afflict and pain people. To crush under His feet all those enclosed in the world. To pervert the judgment of a person before the One above. What should a living person bemoan? Each person for his sins! Who is it that can say something and it becomes so, if Hashem did not command it.*

This first part seems to be crystal clear. Hashem never deliberately causes people to suffer and never deals unfairly with anyone. It is only people's sins that bring about what happens to them. Nothing happens in this world that has not been commanded by Hashem. If there is anything that a person should bemoan, it is his sins, because whatever happens to him is a result of his free-will choices.

In the next verse, however, Chazal make a statement that seems to contradict what was said before:

מִפִּי עֶלְיוֹן לֹא תֵצֵא הָרָעוֹת וְהַטּוֹב:

> *From the mouth of the One on high do not come forth the evils and the good.*

This could be understood to indicate that things that happen to a person are not dictated by Hashem! The following verse, however, reverts

---

10   *Eichah* 3:33–39.

to the original theme—that a person should search through his deeds and do *teshuvah*.

מַה יִּתְאוֹנֵן אָדָם חָי גֶּבֶר חֲטָאָיו: נַחְפְּשָׂה דְרָכֵינוּ וְנַחְקֹרָה וְנָשׁוּבָה עַד ד' נִשָּׂא לְבָבֵנוּ אֶל כַּפָּיִם אֶל ק-ל בַּשָּׁמָיִם:

What should a person complain about? Each person for his sins. Let us search for our sins and return to Hashem. Let us lift our hearts with our hands to G-d in Heaven.

This means that we need to correct our sins and return to our Creator, with heartfelt prayer. But what does the middle verse mean when it says that "the bad and good do not come from the word of the One on high"?

Rashi quotes: "Rabbi Yochanan said: From the day that Hakadosh Baruch Hu said, 'Behold I place before you today life and good, death and evil,' no bad or good comes forth from Him, but the bad and the evil come forth from themselves." This is a very confusing statement. Does it mean that Hashem is not controlling the world?

Absolutely not, as we shall try to explain.

As we have already written, the purpose of life can only be achieved through free will. When we choose well, we are deserving of reward. When we make the wrong choices, we are deserving of punishment. The patterns of reward and punishment are often not visible in this life. Nevertheless, whatever Hashem does is a response to the individual's free will choices or of the free will choices of the community. Therefore, from the moment that free will was ordained, the responses are all predestined in accordance with our actions. The Creator planned out in advance how He would respond to each and every free will action that would ever be perfomed in the world. Of course, it's all coming from Him. It means that when we so something good, or not good, Hashem doesn't have to figure out now how to respond. He already planned in advance all alternatives at the time He ordained free will.

For an illustration, let us take the master chess player. As he studies his opponent's moves, he says to himself: If my opponent moves his knight here, I will respond by moving my rook here. If then he moves his queen, I will move my horse here. On the other hand, if right now he takes a different approach and moves his horse first, then I will do such-and-such in response. He has many different options worked out—many, many moves in advance.

In this same manner, so to speak, we can understand Hakadosh Baruch Hu. What He does is always in response to the free will choices of people, and He has all the numberless options worked out in advance. Certainly, He is doing everything, but when Rabbi Yochanan says that the good and the bad come of themselves, he means that they are already planned out by the Creator in accordance with our choices.

Summing Up

- This world was created for the ultimate purpose of bestowing the ecstasy of *Olam Haba* on the *tzaddikim*.
- The purpose of creation would be frustrated without free will.
- A consistent system of good for the *tzaddik* and bad for the *rasha* would negate free will.
- The difficulties that people go through are part of their tests, to see how they will use their free will to deal with them.
- All accounts are settled in the afterlife. Nothing is overlooked and no one ever gets cheated.

CHAPTER FIVE

When the Wicked Prosper

When we look around, we often see people we would regard as evil but who seem to us to be prospering. As we have said, this causes much confusion in people's minds. Let's see if we can clear the matter up somewhat.

IS THIS THE END? NOT AT ALL!

As previously explained, the basic question of "*rasha v'tov lo*" boils down to: "Do you mean to say that he gets away with all his evil actions and escapes punishment?" The answer is no! No one escapes. No *rasha* ever escaped, and ever will. The worst *resha'im* will be punished forever.[1] Surely Hitler, *yimach shemo*, did not get away scot-free. He is paying for everything he did and will continue paying for all eternity. The *rasha* who lived in tranquility in this world will pay for all of his sins at the time of payment. The tranquility he enjoyed in this world will substitute for any share in the afterlife.

Such has been the *emunah* of Klal Yisrael from time immemorial. No individual ever loses what is coming to him. Some people receive

---

1   See *Rosh Hashanah* 17a and *Rambam, Teshuvah* 3:6, for a list of these people.

it earlier, and some people receive it later, but it all works out fairly in the end.

NOTHING IS OVERLOOKED

The rule is that Hakadosh Baruch Hu doesn't overlook anything, not even the smallest mitzvah, nor the smallest sin. If even a great *tzaddik* commits a small sin, there is an account to be settled. Should a big *rasha* perform a tiny mitzvah, the reward will not be overlooked.

Sometimes we see a *rasha*, a truly evil person, leading a good life. Although he may have transgressed every sin in the Torah, and may be a full-fledged *apikores*, he has a nice house, a seemingly happy family, and money in his pocket. The Torah addressed this problem directly in the *Chumash*. The verse states: "Know that Hashem, your G-d, is Elokim, the trustworthy G-d, who maintains the covenant and the kindness to those who love Him and keep His mitzvos, for a thousand generations."[2] That is for the good ones.

The next verse addresses the *resha'im*: "He pays back those that hate Him to his face to destroy him."[3] *Rashi* quotes Onkelos's translation, that Hashem pays back the *rasha* in **this** world. "He pays back the *rasha*'s good deeds in this world to destroy him from the World to Come." It is as if Hakadosh Baruch Hu is saying to the *rasha*, "I owe you a little something. You did a mitzvah at some point, and I have to pay you for it, but I'm going to pay you in this world. When you get to the afterlife—which is eternal—nothing will be owed to you." It's like throwing his reward in his face and saying, "Here! Just take it." Hakadosh Baruch Hu doesn't want him around in the afterlife, but since Hashem pays all debts, he pays him in this world. Therefore, when you see a *rasha* prospering, don't be envious of him because it may very well mean he will lose out on something infinitely greater and have to pay a big price for it.

---

2   *Devarim* 7:9.
3   *Devarim* 7:10.

IS IT FAIR?

Is it fair to pay the *rasha* in this-worldly currency, when it is virtually valueless compared to next-worldly currency? Imagine the following scenario: The king was in the habit of leaving the palace dressed in the clothes of a commoner. He went swimming in a lake but developed a cramp and was about to drown. There was no one around but a ten-year-old child, who quickly threw him a life preserver, thereby saving his life. When the king came ashore and revived somewhat, he said, "My beloved child! You have saved the life of your king. This afternoon, come to the palace at four o'clock, and I will grant you a reward."

Later that day, the boy arrives at the palace accompanied by his parents. As they enter the throne room, the king rises and comes forth to greet them. He says, "My sweet child, what prize shall I give you for saving the life of your king?" What will a child ask for? Perhaps a new bicycle or a new computer? If his parents have their wits about them, they will advise him to ask the king to defer his reward until he reaches adulthood. Then it will be a different story. He may ask to become the viceroy, or perhaps for the hand of the princess in marriage.

If, however, he asked for the bike, and was given the best and fanciest bike there is, can he still come back at age twenty-five and ask for a reward for saving the king's life? The king will say, "I asked you what you want. You told me your wish, and I gave it to you. I owe you nothing more."

This is precisely the situation with the *rasha*. If he wanted *Olam Haba*, would he be a *rasha*? Hashem is paying him in the currency that he wants, namely, this-worldly benefits. It's not unfair at all.

DON'T FEAR OG

We find numerous examples in *Tanach* of *resha'im* being paid in this world. There were two Emori kings, Sichon and Og, who were conquered by Moshe Rabbeinu and B'nei Yisrael. B'nei Yisrael took their land on the eastern side of the Jordan River, where eventually two and a half tribes settled. After Moshe Rabbeinu had defeated Sichon, Hashem told him not to fear Og. "Don't fear him, for I've given him into your hand,

and you will do to him as you did to Sichon."[4] Concerning Sichon, however, Hashem had never told him not to be afraid. Obviously, Moshe Rabbeinu hadn't been afraid of Sichon. If he had been, Hashem would have encouraged him then, too. Why was Moshe Rabbeinu afraid of Og more than he was afraid of Sichon?

Chazal say that Og had a merit that frightened Moshe Rabbeinu. "He was afraid of the merit in his hand." He had once done a favor for Avraham Avinu. During the war between the four and five kings, Avraham's nephew Lot had been taken captive. Og escaped from the battlefront and came to Avraham to inform him that Lot had been captured. "The refugee came and told Avram."[5] How do we know it was Og? Since it says, *"the* refugee," and not *"a* refugee," we know it is referring to someone the Torah has already identified. Since it later states that Og had escaped from that war, and no other escapee is mentioned, we understand that "the refugee" refers to Og.[6]

So Og told Avraham that Lot had been captured, Avraham dashed into battle, was victorious, and rescued his nephew. This was a very big favor to Avraham. However, the mitzvah that Og did was not nearly as great as it looked. Chazal tell us precisely what Og's intention was in bringing this news: He wanted Avraham to get killed in battle, so that he could take Sarah for himself.[7] This means that Og set his eyes on another man's wife, and in order to have her for himself, he schemed to get Avraham killed. Og's intention was for murder and adultery, and it was more a sin than it was a mitzvah. Nevertheless, Moshe Rabbeinu was afraid of Og because he still deserved some credit for doing something that was of benefit to Avraham. "Maybe the merit of Avraham will stand for him." Perhaps Hakadosh Baruch Hu would not allow Og to be defeated in the *zechus* of the service he had once done for Avraham Avinu.

This begs a question. Wouldn't Moshe Rabbeinu, Aharon HaKohen, Miriam HaNeviah, Nachshon ben Aminadav, the whole tribe of Levi,

---

4   *Devarim* 3:2.
5   *Bereishis* 14:13.
6   *Devarim* 3:11.
7   *Rashi, Bereishis* 14:13; *Bereishis Rabbah* 42:8.

and all of the righteous men and women among Klal Yisrael have had enough merits to outweigh the little mitzvah that Og once did, especially since his intention was evil? Hadn't they done many more well-intentioned mitzvos that would easily outweigh this mitzvah of Og's?

The answer is very simple. B'nei Yisrael surely had plenty of merits! However, it was obvious to Moshe Rabbeinu that Og was receiving his reward in this world. He saw that Og had lived a very long time, a few hundred years since the war in the time of Avraham. He was a giant with great physical prowess. He was mighty, and all the kings paid him tribute (in other words, he had "*protektzia*"). They filled his treasure house with money and Og received much glory. The merits of Klal Yisrael were, of course, millions of times greater than Og's, but their reward was not going to be paid in this world. They would have to wait for *Olam Haba*. Therefore, Moshe Rabbeinu didn't know if he could conquer Og in *Olam Hazeh*. Hakadosh Baruch Hu informed him that Og's time was finally up—he could take him.

NEVUCHADNETZAR'S MITZVAH

Nevuchadnetzar was once a secretary for the king of Bavel.[8] A miracle happened to Chizkiyahu HaMelech, as is told in the books of *Yeshayah*[9] and *Melachim*.[10] As a sign that he would be healed from a fatal illness, Yeshayah HaNavi said that the sun would move backward ten hours for him. This miracle was seen worldwide. When the king of Bavel realized that a miracle had happened, he inquired about it and was told that this was done for Chizkiyahu. The king said that if such a miracle was made for a colleague of his in Eretz Yehudah, he must send him a letter of congratulations. In the royal office, his scribes composed a letter to Chizkiyahu. When they wrote the salutation, however, Nevuchadnetzar was out of the office. When he returned, they had just sent out the letter. Nevchadnezar asked them how they had written the salutation, and they told him that they had written, "Peace to the great King

---

8   *Sanhedrin* 96a.
9   *Yeshayah* 38.
10 *Melachim II* 20:11.

Chizkiyahu, to the great city of Yerushlayim, and to the great G-d of the Jews." Nevuchadnetzar said, "You call Him 'the great G-d,' but you put Him last? It is not respectful of their G-d!" He ran after the messenger, brought back the letter, and corrected it.

Now the Jewish G-d was mentioned first, and they sent out the letter. As a reward for taking three steps—seemingly in honor of Hashem—to call back the messenger, he was granted royalty for three generations: for himself, his son Evil-Merodach, and his grandson Belshatzar. With that power he destroyed the Beis Hamikdash and sent the Jewish People into exile in Bavel. The Gemara says that had he run more than three steps, his reward would have had to be so much greater, nothing would have been left of the Jewish People.[11] Therefore, an angel was sent to stop him after he took three steps.

We see that Hashem's justice is perfect. Nevuchadnetzar, who was a *rasha*, was paid for his good deed in full measure—in this world.

THE TAX COLLECTOR AND THE TALMID CHACHAM

Rashi quotes an amazing story that actually comes from *Talmud Yerushalmi*.[12] In the time of Chazal, the tax collectors were considered absolute *resha'im* because they bought the franchise from the king and extorted money from people by force, taking way above what they had a right to take. The king gave them a police force to help them collect the taxes, and they used this advantage to force the people to pay money that they did not really owe. There was a certain tax collector and an *adam gadol* who both died on the same day, with two concurrent funerals. The whole town came out for the funeral of the *adam gadol*, and only the immediate family came out for the funeral of the tax collector. As the two processions were going to the cemetery, they were attacked. The people had no choice but to put down the two stretchers and run away, leaving the two bodies behind. After things quieted down, the people came back to finish the funerals and inadvertently switched the two bodies. The family of the tax collector took the body of the *talmid*

---

11   *Sanhedrin* 96a.
12   *Sanhedrin* 44b.

chacham, and the people of the city took the body of the tax collector. A *talmid* of the *adam gadol* realized they had made a mistake. He screamed at the people that they had taken the wrong body, but no one listened to him. The family of the tax collector took the body of the *talmid chacham* and buried him in the section of the cemetery reserved for the lowest element of the people, in the grave that had been dug for the tax collector. The body of the tax collector was buried in the honorable spot that had been reserved for the *adam gadol*. The *talmid* of the *adam gadol* was beside himself, and in his distress he fell asleep.

His *rebbi* appeared to him in a dream. The *rebbi* said, "Don't be upset! Come with me, and let me show you my glorious place in Gan Eden." In the dream, he showed the *talmid* his incredibly magnificent place in Gan Eden. Then the *rebbi* said, "Now let me show you the place of the *rasha* in Gehinnom." What he showed him there was a very unpleasant scene. The *talmid* said to the *rebbi*, "If it is true that you were such a *tzaddik gamur*, and deserving of such a glorious place in Gan Eden, why is it that you were buried in such disgrace? And why is it that the *rasha*, who was so wicked and deserving of such punishment in Gehinnom, was buried with the utmost dignity?" The *rebbi* said, "I was indeed a *tzaddik gamur*, but one time I heard people speaking disparagingly about a *talmid chacham*, and I didn't protest. I should have stood up for the *kavod* of the *talmid chacham*, but I didn't. Therefore, my *kavod* was also diminished, so at the time of my funeral, I was buried in disgrace. That was my punishment. The *rasha*, on the other hand, hardly ever did a good thing in his life. Once, however, he invited the mayor of the city to a catered dinner, and the mayor never showed up. He was left with a large amount of uneaten food, so he dispersed it to the poor. For that one mitzvah, the *rasha* got the reward of being buried with dignity. My punishment was given to me in this world, and the *rasha*'s reward was also given to him in this world."

A LITTLE MITZVAH

Rabbi Elchonon Wasserman related a story about his *rebbi*, the holy Chafetz Chaim. The Chafetz Chaim needed to write a letter to an editor whom he considered to be a *rasha*. The Chafetz Chaim was in a quandary. After all, when writing a letter asking for a favor, there is no alternative but to write some sort of respectful salutation. However, it is a very big sin to give *kavod* to a *rasha*! The Chafetz Chaim struggled to figure out how to write it in such a manner as to give the *rasha* the least possible amount of *kavod*. For days, the Chafetz Chaim put off sending out the letter. Finally, he decided what he thought would be the minimum *kavod* that he could get away with. Even after he sent off the letter, he was still very concerned that he may have given the *rasha* too much *kavod*. Years later, Rav Elchonon came to the Chafetz Chaim and told him that the very same *rasha* had been made guest of honor at a dinner of a *frum* institution. The Chafetz Chaim sighed and said, "Who knows? Maybe he once said, '*Amen yehei shemei rabbah*,' so he's being paid his reward."

Summing Up

- No one ever gains from transgressing the will of Hashem. The evil man's prosperity is not a benefit for him. It will be deducted from any portion of *Olam Haba* coming to him.
- The Torah teaches us this principle explicitly, in no uncertain terms.

CHAPTER SIX

Yissurim of the Righteous Are Not for Naught

No explanations will make *yissurim* hurt less than they do. A toothache is a toothache, poverty is poverty. Disappointments in life are painful, and nothing that we write here can change that, at least in the physical sense.

Intellectually, gaining a perspective on our travails can at least offer comfort and peace of mind, knowing that what we suffer is not in vain. Internalizing this on an emotional level is much harder and will take much longer, but that is not a reason to refrain from first learning and absorbing what our Torah has told us about the purpose of human suffering.

THERE ARE REASONS

Our *mesorah* tells us that *yissurim* are brought for very positive purposes. Just as everything that happens in the world comes from Hakadosh Baruch Hu, so too, no *yissurim* come upon a person without the exact judgment of Hakadosh Baruch Hu. Even if a person merely

63

bangs his finger accidentally on the corner of a table, there was a special session of the Heavenly Court at which it was decided that he needed to bang his finger. "No one bangs his finger below [in this world], unless they decree it upon him above."[1]

In the following chapters we will endeavor to outline a number of such reasons, as explained in the words of Chazal.

Our *emunah* also teaches us that Hakadosh Baruch Hu has only our good at heart, and He does only what He knows needs to be done. Imagine someone who knows nothing about surgery walking into an operating room just as the surgeon is cutting a limb off a person. He would undoubtedly be shocked to the core, and surely perceive it as nothing less than wicked cruelty. One who understands, however, knows that the doctor is actually doing the person a tremendous favor. He is saving his life from an infection that would have spread and killed him. There was no alternative other than to perform an amputation, which the patient himself begged him to do. It is precisely in this manner that we must perceive the sufferings of this world. Hashem brings travails only when He knows that they are necessary. We, however, view this entire matter and make judgments based only on what we see with our limited this-worldly eyes. We simply can't see past the comforts of our existence and what we are familiar with in this world. Superficially, this-worldly good seems good and this-worldly bad seems bad. Although this is not true—and the opposite is often the case—it is hard to see it any other way. That's why we understand so little.

TESHUVAH

The first reason why a good person may undergo *yissurim* is to arouse him to do *teshuvah*. (Later, we will devote an entire chapter to the subject of *teshuvah*.) After all, if we do *teshuvah* properly, our *aveiros* are erased retroactively.

---

1   *Chullin* 7b.

DEBTS TO PAY

We read in *Koheles*: "There is no one in the world so righteous that he does only good and never sins."[2] Therefore, even a *tzaddik* has some bills that must be paid, either in this world or in the next. Hashem's attribute of Divine justice requires that no deed ever goes unnoticed. Everything is put on the Heavenly scale. If that's the case, then every *tzaddik* must eventually undergo some small amount of retribution before he can receive the multitude of reward that he deserves for his *maasim tovim*. Since the *onesh* (punishment) in the afterlife is infinitely greater than the suffering one goes through in this world, when Hakadosh Baruch Hu chooses to give a *tzaddik* his *onesh* in this world, it's actually a big favor. It is definitely not something a person would necessarily wish upon himself; nevertheless, it is considerably better to receive punishment in this temporary world than to receive it in *Olam Haba*!

A BARGAIN IN RETROSPECT

Many people willingly sacrifice years of their lives training for a career. Most of those years are spent in constant studying for tests and working on assignments. For example, it takes years and years to become a doctor. One must graduate university, medical school, and complete an internship and residency, often having to work all night; it's a colossal workload. Finally, after giving up years of their life, it's time to open up a practice, earn a good living—even become wealthy—and hopefully do what they longed to do. People make big sacrifices—even undergo suffering for a while—in order to arrive at some goal which, in their eyes, justifies the sacrifice that they have made. Ask them later if it was worth it, and most will give an emphatic yes.

In a similar vein, Chazal tell us that as painful as *yissurim* may be, they accomplish great things for a person vis-à-vis *Olam Haba*. If we could ask the *neshamos* in Gan Eden if it is worth it, they would respond enthusiastically that it is a bargain.

---

2   *Koheles* 7:20.

WAKE UP AND DO TESHUVAH

Some *yissurim* are for the purpose of arousing a person to do *teshuvah*. The Gemara says that "when a person sees *yissurim* coming upon him, he should start looking through his deeds"[3] to see if there is something he needs to do *teshuvah* for. The *Navi* says that when Hashem brings punishment and we don't get the message, then the *yissurim* are for naught. "For naught I smote your children. They took no *mussar* lesson."[4] The purpose of the *yissurim* is that we should learn lessons and do *teshuvah*. If we don't pay attention, then the suffering we went through—which was intended as a favor to us—served no purpose. What a wasted opportunity!

HOW PRECIOUS ARE YISSURIM

Menasheh was one of the most wicked kings to ever reign over the land of Yehudah. He coerced the people to worship idols, murdered the *nevi'im* who spoke out against him, and even killed his own grandfather Yeshayah HaNavi. He corrupted the people so thoroughly that even in the time of his righteous grandson Yoshiyahu, there was retribution for his sins: "But Hashem had not turned from his burning anger on Yehudah for the angering things that Menasheh had angered Him."[5] Furthermore, the destruction of the First Beis Hamikdash and Yerushalayim is attributed to him: "I will cause all the kingdoms of the earth to tremble because of what Menasheh, son of Chizkiyahu, did in Yerushalayim."[6]

His story is most instructive. From it, we will learn both the power of *teshuvah* and the benefit of *yissurim*.

Incredibly, after going through a trauma, Menasheh actually did *teshuvah*. He removed all the idols in Eretz Yehudah and instructed the entire Jewish People to return to Hashem. Yet, although Menasheh did *teshuvah*, there is still a dispute as to whether his *teshuvah* was accepted.

---

3   *Berachos* 5a.
4   *Yirmiyahu* 2:30.
5   *Melachim II* 23:26.
6   *Yirmiyahu* 15:4.

The Mishnah includes Menasheh in the list of kings who lost their share in *Olam Haba*.

> *Three kings and four commoners have no share in Olam Haba. Three kings: Yeravam, Achav, and Menasheh. Rabbi Yehudah says Menasheh does have a share in Olam Haba, for the verse says: "He prayed to Him, He heard his supplication and brought him back to Yerushalayim to his kingdom." They said: "He was brought back to his kingdom, but not to his share in Olam Haba."*[7]

Rabbi Yochanan gives a final decision about the matter. Menasheh's *teshuvah* was indeed accepted, and he does have a share in *Olam Haba*: "Whoever says that Menasheh has no share in *Olam Haba* weakens [discourages] the hands of *baalei teshuvah*."[8]

The Gemara provides us with an amazing insight.[9] When Rabbi Eliezer became sick, his students came to visit. Each one told him how precious he was to them, until it was Rabbi Akiva's turn. Rabbi Akiva told him that suffering is precious. (It is astounding that Rabbi Akiva said this while Rabbi Eliezer was sick and suffering, lying on his deathbed.) Let us look at the Gemara:

> *When Rabbi Eliezer became sick, four sages came to visit him: Rabbi Tarfon, Rabbi Yehoshua, Rabbi Elazar ben Azariah, and Rabbi Akiva.*
>
> *Rabbi Tarfon said, "You are better for Yisrael than the raindrops. Raindrops are only in this world, Rebbi is in this world and in Olam Haba."*
>
> *Rabbi Yehoshua said, "You are better for Yisrael than the ball of the sun. The ball of the sun is only in this world, Rebbi is in this world and in Olam Haba."*

---

7   *Sanhedrin* 90a.
8   *Sanhedrin* 103a.
9   *Sanhedrin* 101a.

> Rabbi Elazar ben Azariah said, "You are better for Yisrael than a mother and father. Mother and father are only in this world, Rebbi is in this world and in Olam Haba."
>
> Rabbi Akiva said, "Suffering is precious." He [Rabbi Eliezer] said, "Support me, so I can hear the words of my student Akiva, who said that suffering is precious. Akiva! From where have you learned this?"
>
> Rabbi Akiva said, "Rebbi, I learned it from a verse. It says: 'Menasheh was twelve years old when he took over the throne, and he reigned for fifty-five years. He did what was evil in Hashem's eyes.'[10] And it is written: 'Also these are the proverbs of Shlomo, which the men of Chizkiyahu Melech Yehudah recorded.'[11] Do you think that Chizkiyahu Melech Yehudah taught the whole world Torah and he didn't teach his son Menasheh? From all the work that Chizkiyahu put into Menasheh, he couldn't turn him to be good. The only thing that could turn him to good was suffering, as it says: 'Hashem spoke to Menasheh and his people, but they did not listen. He brought upon them the officers of the king of Ashur. Menasheh was captured by the king of Ashur with hunting hooks, who tied him in chains and led him away to Bavel.'[12] And it says: 'When he was in distress, he beseeched Hashem and humbled himself very much before the G-d of his fathers, and he davened to Him. Hashem heard Menasheh's supplication and responded to him, and He returned Menasheh to Yerushalayim to his kingdom. Menasheh knew that Hashem is Elokim.'[13] So, from here you learn that suffering is precious."

Rabbi Akiva's teaching was not just for Rabbi Eliezer; it is for all of us, and it is life-changing.

---

10 *Melachim II* 21:1.
11 *Mishlei* 25:1.
12 *Divrei Hayamim II* 33:10–11.
13 *Divrei Hayamim II* 33:12.

MENASHEH IN HOT WATER

The *Talmud Yerushalmi*[14] tells us what happened to Menasheh on that fateful trip to Ashur, when he was led away in chains as a lowly prisoner.

> *Rabbi Levi said, they made for him a cauldron of copper, put him inside it and lit the fire underneath. Once he saw how much trouble he was in, he did not leave out one idol in the world to which he did not call. When it didn't help him at all, he said, "I remember that my father read me this verse in shul: 'When you are in distress and all these things have found you, you shall return to Hashem, your G-d, and listen to His voice. Hashem is a merciful and gracious G-d, He will not let you go or destroy you, nor forget the covenant with your forefathers which He swore to them.'*[15]*"*

Finally, Menasheh cracked and submitted himself to his Creator. He promised that if Hashem would redeem him and restore him to his kingdom, he would spread Hashem's name to the entire Jewish People and endeavor to undo all the harm that he had done.

> *When he was in distress, he pleaded before Hashem, his G-d, and humbled himself very much before the G-d of his fathers. He prayed to him and Hashem responded to him, heard his supplication, and returned him to Yerushalayim to his kingdom. Menasheh knew that Hashem is [truly] G-d.*[16]

His prayer and *teshuvah* were accepted, and he ultimately was awarded a share in *Olam Haba*.

Had Menasheh been asked in advance if he would like to be put in a cauldron of boiling water, the answer would have been an emphatic "No!" In truth, however, Hakadosh Baruch Hu did him a tremendous favor by bringing on him terrible fright, disgrace, and physical suffering

---

14 *Yerushalmi, Sanhedrin Perek Chelek, halachah 2.*
15 *Devarim 4:30.*
16 *Divrei Hayamim II 32:12.*

because this is what led him to *teshuvah* and, ultimately, to his eternal destination—*Olam Haba*.

Summing Up

Yissurim hurt. We don't want them, and we often ask Hashem not to bring them upon us. Nevertheless, when they come, one of their benefits is that they are a great awakening to do *teshuvah*. If we indeed do *teshuvah*, we will merit *Olam Haba*, which is our destination.

CHAPTER
SEVEN

Yissurim for Atonement

There is a second possible reason for *yissurim*. Not only do *yissurim* arouse a person to do *teshuvah*, but the suffering we go through in this world actually helps us to atone for our sins. Since the purpose of this life is merely to serve as a corridor to *Olam Haba*, the more atonement we have in this world, the less atonement we will require in the afterlife. Rabbi Shimon ben Lakish said: "It says [the word] *bris* concerning salt[1] and it says the word *bris* concerning *yissurim*.[2] Just as the salt sweetens the meat, so too do *yissurim* atone for sins."[3]

SOMETIMES TESHUVAH ALONE WILL NOT SUFFICE

There are certain severe sins for which *teshuvah* alone is not a complete atonement. Negative commandments that bear a punishment of *kares* or death by *beis din* require *teshuvah*, Yom Kippur, and *yissurim*.

---

1 That Hashem made a covenant with the earthly waters that they would go onto the *korbanos* on the Altar in the form of salt.
2 In the portion of the *Tochachah*, where the Torah forecasts what will befall the Jewish People if they stray from the path of Torah.
3 *Berachos* 5a.

Rabbi Masya ben Charash asked Rabbi Elazar ben Azariah in Rome: "Did you hear the four divisions of atonement about which Rabbi Yishmael taught?" He said, "There are [really] only three, with teshuvah accompanying each one:

- If a person transgressed a positive commandment and did teshuvah, he doesn't budge from there until he is forgiven.
- If he transgressed a negative commandment and did teshuvah, the teshuvah suspends the atonement and Yom Kippur is the final atonement.
- If someone transgressed a sin of kares or a sin liable to the death penalty in court, teshuvah and Yom Kippur suspend the atonement, and yissurim bring the final atonement.
- But for a person who committed a chillul Hashem, neither teshuvah, Yom Kippur, or yissurim can atone, but all of them suspend the atonement and death completes the atonement.[4]

We never deliberately afflict ourselves. When a person needs to undergo *yissurim*, it is Hashem Who decides what the nature of the affliction will be, and how severe it will be.

WHY ISN'T TESHUVAH SUFFICIENT?

Why is it that *teshuvah* is not sufficient for some sins? Rabbeinu Yonah explains that this can be likened to a garment with a deep stain, which needs numerous washings. The first wash will take out the surface part of the stain, but the stain will still be embedded in the garment and require numerous additional washings. For these sins, *yissurim* can take out the remaining part of the stain, and the *neshamah* becomes completely clean.

> Behold! There are many levels to teshuvah. According to the levels, the person will come close to Hakadosh Baruch Hu. Truthfully, for every teshuvah there is forgiveness. However,

---

4   *Yoma* 86a.

the nefesh will not become pure with a total purity, so that the sins shall be as if they never were, unless the person purifies his heart and prepares his spirit…Just as a garment that needs to be washed, a little washing will remove the dirt, but [if it is a deep stain,] only with a lot of washing will the garment turn white again.[5]

SUFFERING AS A FAVOR

While we should pray to avoid suffering, when it does happen, Rabbeinu Yonah teaches us that a person should realize that his suffering was given to him as a favor, for which he must be grateful.

> You should know and understand that the chastisement of Hashem, may He be blessed, is for the benefit of the person. For if a person sinned before Him and did what was evil in His eyes, Hashem's chastisement comes upon him for two purposes. One is to atone for his sins and to remove his iniquity. With the illnesses and afflictions of the body which Hashem inflicts upon him, He will heal the sickness of his soul. Sin is the sickness of the soul. As David said, "Heal my soul because I have sinned to you." The second is to remind him and to cause him to repent from his evil ways.[6]

Rabbeinu Yonah[7] quotes further from Chazal:

> Our Sages of blessed memory said: "Rabbi Eliezer ben Yaakov says, 'As long as a person dwells in tranquility, none of his sins are being atoned for, but through suffering he becomes acceptable to Hakadosh Baruch Hu.'[8] As it states: 'The one Hashem loves, He rebukes as a father [does] to a son whom he [still] desires.'[9]"

---

5 Shaarei Teshuvah 1:9.
6 Shaarei Teshuvah 2:3.
7 Shaarei Teshuvah 2:4.
8 Sifri, Devarim 5:6.
9 Mishlei 3:12.

This means that the son appeases the father who has rebuked him, as long as the father has not given up on him.

DON'T GET DISCOURAGED

In *Koheles*, Shlomo HaMelech advises us not to get discouraged when the going gets rough, but to realize that it is all for a very important purpose: "If the spirit of the ruler rises against you, don't leave your place, for the healing will remove great sins."[10] *Rashi* explains: "If the spirit of the ruler of the world [Hakadosh Baruch Hu] is being exacting on you with the *middas ha'din*, don't leave your place, [meaning,] don't leave your good behavior and say, 'What does all my righteousness do for me?' The exactness of the judgment with the *yissurim* that come on you is a healing for your sins and will remove from you great sins." When Hashem is being very strict with you, realize that it is for a great purpose of healing: to remove your sins.

WAYS TO AVOID YISSURIM

There are things we can do to avoid the suffering for our sins.[11] Consider two basic ideas:

- Giving charity can enable one to be spared from death, and certainly from other *yissurim*. Other forms of kind deeds offer even greater power than *tzedakah*: "Performance of kind deeds is greater than charity."[12]
- By exerting ourselves in the service of Hakadosh Baruch Hu and investing toil in the study of Torah. So says the midrash: "If a person transgressed a sin for which there is a punishment of *kares* or death in *beis din*, if he was accustomed to learning one chapter a day, he should now learn two chapters a day." Rabbeinu Yonah explains this midrash as follows:

   This will protect him from the yissurim in two ways. One, because our Sages have told us, "Learning Torah is equal to all [the other

---

10 *Koheles* 10:4.
11 *Shaarei Teshuvah* 4:11.
12 *Sukkah* 49:2.

mitzvos put together]."[13] *The second, because when he puts in toil in Torah and exerts himself in it, and moves away the sleep from his eyes [staying up late and learning], this will count for him in the place of yissurim. As our Sages have said, "All people were made to toil. Fortunate is the one whose toil is in Torah."*[14] *They also said, "Why is Torah called tushiya? Because it weakens a person's energy."*[15]

WITH KINDNESS AND TRUTH

There is a statement in *Mishlei*: "With kindness and truth, sin will be atoned, and with the fear of Hashem by turning away from evil."[16] Rabbeinu Yonah comments:

Contemplate the hidden meaning of this verse. It is certainly true that if the sinner did not repent for his sins, his deeds will not be atoned for with acts of kindness. As the verse in the Torah says: "[Hashem] will not show favoritism or accept a bribe."[17] *The Sages of blessed memory said, "He will not accept a bribe of mitzvos to forgive and overlook sins." They also said, "Whoever says that Hashem forgoes things, He will forgo his life." Shlomo HaMelech was really speaking [in that verse] about a person who had done teshuvah. There are some sins for which teshuvah and Yom Kippur [are not sufficient], and the sin is still pending until yissurim will finally cleanse them...Behold, the kindness [that one does] will protect the sinner and guard him from the yissurim, and certainly from death, as it is written: "Charity will save from death."*[18]

---

13 *Pe'ah* 1:1.
14 *Sanhedrin* 99b.
15 *Sanhedrin* 26b.
16 *Mishlei* 16:6.
17 *Yalkut Mishlei* 947.
18 *Shaarei Teshuvah* 1:47.

Summing Up

- Another benefit of *yissurim* is that they atone for the more severe sins that require more than just *teshuvah*.
- The more atonement we get in this world, the better off we will be in the next.

CHAPTER
EIGHT

Yissurim and Prayer

Our Creator wants us to connect with Him while we are in this world. The more we connect with Him here, the more we will be able to connect with Him in the next world. One of the best ways to do this is through the mode of prayer. The Gemara tells us that *tefillah* is one of the most important things we can ever do, but we must take it seriously: "One of the *Rabbanan* said to Rav Bevai bar Abaye…'What is the meaning of the verse, "As is the height so is the cheapness to people?"' He said to him, 'These are the things which stand in the highest place in the world but people treat them lightly.'"[1] He was referring to *tefillah*.

EVERYTHING WAITED FOR TEFILLAH

> *Rav Asi posed a contradiction: In one verse it says that the earth gave forth the plants on the third day. But it is also written: "All the shrubs of the field had not yet sprouted" on Erev Shabbos. This teaches us that the plants came out [of the ground] and stood by the opening of the ground until the first*

---

1   Berachos 7b.

man came and asked for mercy for them. The rains fell and they sprouted forth. To teach you that Hashem longs for the prayers of tzaddikim.[2]

In other words, the completion of the entire Creation had to wait for Adam's *tefillah* because Hashem longed to hear his *tefillah*. *Tefillah*, talking and connecting to Hashem, is one of the things that we came to this world to do. Davening for something is a way of showing that we recognize that Hashem is the One Who gives it to us; we thereby internalize this recognition into our *neshamos*.

HASHEM WAITS FOR OUR TEFILLOS

Sometimes difficulties are brought on a person to arouse him to pray. The Avos and Imahos (with the exception of Leah) were all childless for many long years. They davened fervently that the Ribbono Shel Olam should give them children. It was a very distressing time in their lives. Their longing for children was not merely for the sake of having a baby upon whom to shower their affection; they desired children in order to fulfill their life's mission, which was to establish a nation that would be completely devoted to the service of Hashem. After the war with the four kings, Hashem promised Avraham Avinu great reward. Avraham responded, "Hashem! What can You give me if I have no children?" What he meant was that nothing else meant anything to him, so desperately did our forbearers desire children. Yet, Hashem decreed that it was not yet time, and the Avos and Imahos each suffered through long periods of waiting.

Why? "Rabbi Yitzchak said: Why were our forefathers childless? Because Hakadosh Baruch Hu longs for the prayers of the *tzaddikim*."[3] Of course, Hashem lacks nothing. He does not need their prayers, but it is for the benefit of the *tzaddik*, who becomes greater and closer to Hakadosh Baruch Hu through prayer. When Hakadosh Baruch Hu felt

---

2   *Chullin* 60b, quoted by *Rashi* in *Bereishis* 2:5.
3   *Yevamos* 64a.

that they had grown and developed enough through their *tefillos*, He gave them children.

KEEP DAVENING, EVEN AFTER THINGS GET BETTER

As human nature often dictates, when people are in distress they turn to Hashem for help. When things get better, they stop. Like the person who was on his way to an important business meeting and desperately needed a parking space. He turned to Hashem and said, "Ribbono Shel Olam, please help me find a parking space!" At that moment the person right in front of him pulled out of a space. He said, "Never mind, G-d, I found one myself!" We seem to forget our dependence on Hakadosh Baruch Hu as soon as things get better.

The midrash teaches us a similar lesson. As long as B'nei Yisrael were enslaved in Egypt, they prayed and cried out constantly to Hakadosh Baruch Hu to help them. When, finally, Moshe Rabbeinu came along and they were relieved from their distress, they stopped davening. The midrash applies a verse from *Shir Hashirim* to that situation: "Let Me hear your voice because your voice is sweet."[4] Hashem was waiting for them to daven again because "He longs for the prayers of *tzaddikim*." He therefore orchestrated their distress at the Yam Suf, with the Egyptians pursuing them from behind and the sea blocking them in front. There was nowhere to run, so finally they cried out to Hashem. Hashem said, "That's all I wanted, just to hear your voice. Now the Yam Suf can split."

Here are the words of the midrash:

> *Why did Hashem do so to them? Only because Hakadosh Baruch Hu was longing for their prayers. Rabbi Yehoshua ben Levi said, "To what can this be compared? To a king that was going on the road and a princess was crying out, 'Please, your majesty! Save me from the robbers [who are attacking me].' The king listened and saved her. After some time, he wanted to marry her, he wanted [at least] that she should speak with him, but she did not want to. What did the king do? He sent*

---

4   *Shir Hashirim* 2:14.

'robbers' upon her, and she once again cried out to him. He said, 'That's what I was longing for, just to hear your voice.' So it was with Yisrael. As long as they were in Egypt and were being enslaved, they cried out and directed their eyes to Heaven. As it says: 'In those many days…and B'nei Yisrael cried out, and their outcry went up to Hashem from their labor.' Immediately 'Hashem saw the [distress of] B'nei Yisrael' and began to take them out from there with a strong hand and an outstretched arm. Hashem wanted to hear their voice another time, but they didn't want to. What did He do? He incited Pharaoh to chase after them, as it says: 'And Pharaoh approached.' Immediately 'B'nei Yisrael cried out to Hashem.' Hakadosh Baruch Hu said, 'That's what I wanted, to hear your voice.' As it says: 'My dove in the cracks of the rocks, let me hear your voice.' It means, 'Let me hear the voice that I already heard in Mitzrayim.' Therefore, it says, 'Let me hear your voice.' Once they davened, Hakadosh Baruch Hu said to Moshe, 'Why are you standing and davening? My children's prayer has already preceded your prayer,' as it says: 'Why are you crying out to me?'"[5]

Summing Up

Sometimes we are afflicted in order to arouse us to sincere *tefillah*, which we may have been neglecting.

---

5   *Shemos Rabbah* 21:5.

CHAPTER NINE

Great Gifts, but Only through Yissurim

We have been taught that Torah, Eretz Yisrael, and *Olam Haba* can only be acquired through *yissurim*: "Rabbi Shimon ben Yochai says: Hakadosh Baruch Hu gave three good presents to the Jewish People; all of them were only given through *yissurim*. The three gifts are: Torah, Eretz Yisrael, and *Olam Haba*."[1]

YISSURIM FOR TORAH

There are many sources that show that Torah is acquired only through *yissurim*.

"[From where do we know that] Torah learning [can only be acquired through *yissurim*]? Because it says in the verse: 'How fortunate is the person whom You afflict, Hashem, and You teach him Your Torah.'" It was no simple thing for Klal Yisrael to receive the Torah. They had to go through incredibly difficult enslavement in Egypt in order to

---

1   *Berachos* 5a.

become sufficiently purified and worthy of becoming the Torah nation: "Hashem took you and brought you out of the iron smelting pot, from Egypt, to be to Him a nation of inheritance as this very day."[2]

The experience at Har Sinai was so traumatic that B'nei Yisrael pleaded with Moshe Rabbeinu not to have to undergo such an experience again.[3] That was what we needed to go through initially just to receive the Torah in the first place. Forever after, learning Torah requires one to undergo hardship.

We are commanded to continue learning till the very day of death, otherwise we may forget the learning we have already acquired: "Until when is a person obligated to learn Torah? Until the day of his death, as it says: 'Lest they depart from your heart all the days of your life.' Whenever a person is not involved in learning, he forgets."[4]

The Torah is described as "longer than an expansive land, wider than the sea."[5] We never finish, and we must constantly review.

A life of luxury or indulgence is in conflict with amassing Torah knowledge. One must be willing to endure deprivation in order to become a *talmid chacham*: "Such is the way of Torah: eat bread with salt, drink a little water, sleep on the ground, live a life of privation, and labor in the Torah. If you do so, how fortunate you will be, and it will be good for you. Fortunate in this world, and good for you in *Olam Haba*."[6]

The Tanna Rabbi Nehorai tells us: "Go into exile to a place of Torah. Do not say that it will follow you, that your colleagues will maintain it in your hand, do not rely on your own understanding."[7] In order to grow in Torah learning, one needs the atmosphere of great *talmidei chachamim* and their students. In times gone by, there were no *kollelim* such as we have today. Someone who wanted to devote himself to studying Torah, without the distractions of home and family, would go into exile to

---

2   *Devarim* 4:20.
3   *Shemos* 20:15–16.
4   Rambam, *Talmud Torah* 1:10.
5   *Iyov* 11:9.
6   *Avos* 6:4.
7   *Avos* 4:14.

learn in a different city. This was a common practice and exemplifies the sacrifices that one must make to become great in Torah.

Learning well is hard work, and many learn until late at night. Sometimes a person does not even sleep at night because they are thinking about a difficult piece in their learning. It is a big labor, involving unique *yissurim*. We already quoted from *Shaarei Teshuvah* that the toil one puts into learning can replace the *yissurim* needed to atone for one's sins. Torah is indeed "sweeter than honey and honeycombs."[8] However, the path to that great pleasure is uphill all the way, with much effort and toil to make the climb.

YISSURIM FOR ERETZ YISRAEL

"[From where do we know that] Eretz Yisrael [can only be acquired through *yissurim*]? Because it says in the verse: 'As a man afflicts his son, Hashem afflicts you,'[9] and shortly afterward it says: 'Hashem is bringing you to a good land.'[10]"

All the travails B'nei Yisrael went through in Egypt and in the *midbar* were a preparation for their entry into Eretz Yisrael. After they entered, there were seven years of war, followed by seven years of dividing up the land. All that time, the people were unsettled.

YISSURIM FOR OLAM HABA

"[From where do we know that] *Olam Haba* [can only be acquired through *yissurim*]? Because it is written: "A mitzvah is a candle, Torah is the light, and the way to eternal life is [through] the chastisement of *mussar*."[11]

No one can sit back and relax—and yet expect to get to *Olam Haba*. It requires a lifetime of toil, and it's not an easy path that's strewn with roses. Part of the program is to go through life's difficulties and overcome them. As already stated, every situation in life poses a *nisayon* for the individual. The hard knocks are one type of test; the easy, good times are another.

---

8   *Tehillim* 19:11.
9   *Devarim* 8:5.
10   *Devarim* 8:7.
11   *Mishlei* 6:23.

CHAPTER
TEN

All for the Good

Our chachamim have taught us to view everything that Hashem does with a positive attitude, even when it is something we would consider bad.

> Rav Huna said in the name of Rav, in the name of Rabbi Meir, and also we learned this in the name of Rabbi Akiva, that a person should always be accustomed to saying that whatever Hashem does is for the good. As this [following] story, that Rabbi Akiva was once traveling on the road. He came to a certain town, and when he asked for lodging, no one was willing to give him a place to stay. He said, "Whatever Hashem does, He does for the good." He spent the night outdoors. He had with him a rooster, a donkey, and a candle. A gust of wind blew out the candle. A cat came and ate up the rooster. A lion came along and devoured the donkey. He said, "Whatever Hashem does, He does for the good." That night a troop of Romans came through the town and captured it. Rabbi Akiva said, "You see? I told you everything Hashem does is for the good."[1]

As *Rashi* explains: "If I would have had a light, the troop would have seen it. If the rooster would have crowed, or if the donkey had brayed, the

---

1   *Berachos* 60b.

troop would have come and captured me."[2] In other words, Rabbi Akiva escaped because of the seeming misfortune he underwent beforehand. Sometimes we see it subsequently, and sometimes we don't. Either way, a person should always be accustomed to saying, "Everything that Hashem does is for the good."

THE TRUE JUDGE

The *berachah* for good news is *"Ha'tov V'Ha'meitiv*—[Blessed is Hashem,] Who is good and does good." The *berachah* for bad news is *"Dayan Ha'emes*—[Blessed is Hashem,] Who is the true Judge."

The Mishnah states: "Just as we make a blessing over good news, so do we make a blessing over bad news."[3] The Gemara questions the words "just as." It could just as easily have said, "We make a blessing over good news, and we make a blessing over bad news."

Rava explains: "We must accept bad news with *simchah* [just as when we receive good tidings]."[4] As *Rashi* explains: "Just as we thank Hashem with *simchah* when we receive good news, so must we accept bad news with *simchah* and 'make the blessing with a full heart.'" It is not that we are expected to *prefer* bad news over good news, but if this is what Hashem has given us, we must accept it without complaint.

"REBBI, IT'S SIMPLE"

When the Beis HaLevi was a Rav in Slutzk, Poland, there was a certain wealthy member of the community who had an import and export business. The manager who supervised his affairs came to the Beis HaLevi and said, *"Rebbi*, I just received a telegram that my boss's biggest ship sank at sea. Basically, that means he is now bankrupt. I simply don't know how to give him this telegram because I don't know what it will do to him." The Beis HaLevi said, "Leave the telegram here, and send your boss to me." The boss came to the Rav and peeked over the Beis HaLevi's shoulder. He noticed that the Rav was learning the ninth *perek* of *Berachos*—a relatively easy *perek*—full of stories and *mussar*.

---

2   Berachos 60b.
3   Berachos 54a.
4   Berachos 60a.

The Beis HaLevi's brow was furrowed, as if he was perplexed, trying to understand something very difficult.

The *baal ha'bayis* asked, "What is the *Rebbi* finding so difficult in the ninth *perek* of *Berachos*?"

The Rav answered, "I just can't understand. The Gemara says that when you make the *berachah* of *Dayan Ha'emes*, you should do so *b'simchah*, with joy. How is it possible for a person to accept suffering with joy?"

The *baal ha'bayis* said, "*Rebbi*, it's simple! If you know that everything Hashem does is for your good, you can accept it with joy."

When the Beis HaLevi handed him the telegram, the poor fellow fainted on the spot. When he was revived, he said to the Beis HaLevi, "*Rebbi*, you saved my life. If you hadn't helped me bring out that thought just before I read the telegram, I don't know if I would have survived."

ON THAT DAY...

As already mentioned, there is a blessing that one says when one gets bad news. For any misfortune, such as upon the death of a loved one, or if a person hears that his business has been wiped out, he recites the blessing *Dayan Ha'emes*, that "Hashem is the True Judge." On the other hand, for good tidings, he says, *Ha'tov V'Ha'meitiv*, "Thank You, Hashem, for being good to me and to others." The Gemara tells us an amazing thought. The blessing *Dayan Ha'emes* is the one we say now, before the ultimate *geulah*. However, when Mashiach comes, we will conduct ourselves differently.

The Gemara asks a question on the verse from *Zechariah*: "Hashem will be king over all the earth. On that day Hashem will be One and His name will be One."[5]

> Do you think that today He is not One? Rabbi Acha bar Chanina said, "Not like this world is the World to Come. In this world, for good tidings we say [the blessing] Ha'tov V'Ha'meitiv, on

---

5   *Zechariah* 14:9.

bad tidings we say [the blessing] Dayan Ha'emes. In the World to Come, everything will be Ha'tov V'Ha'meitiv.[6]

Hence, we learn that bad news—for example, a big loss—is intrinsically, in the world of truth, just as positive as the good news that we have won the multimillion-dollar lottery. The Sages understood that it would be unrealistic to expect us to feel that way in this world and therefore did not insist that we do so. We are not presently able to say *Ha'tov V'Ha'meitiv* on bad news. All we can say is *"Baruch Dayan Ha'emes,"* i.e., I accept Your judgment. But in Messianic times, our recognition of Hashem's goodness in all He does will be so deep and all penetrating that we will be able to say *Ha'tov V'Ha'meitiv* even for bad news.

ALL FROM ONE SOURCE

Every day we recite, "Hear o'Israel, Hashem is our G-d [*Elokeinu*], Hashem is One."[7] Each of Hashem's names signifies a specific aspect of how Hashem deals with the world. The name "Hashem" refers to the attribute of mercy, while the name "*Elokeinu*" refers to the attribute of Divine justice and punishment. In this verse, the name Hashem is written twice, once before the name *Elokeinu*, and once after. The *Malbim* offers an amazing insight on this verse:

> *The verse shortly before Shema is about fearing Hashem: "In order that you shall fear Hashem, your G-d."*
>
> *The verse after Shema is about loving Hashem: "You shall love Hashem, your G-d."*
>
> *Generally, the one you fear you won't love, and the one you love you won't fear. Here, the Torah commands us to do both: to have both fear and love of Hashem. The verse of Shema in between clarifies how we can be expected to have seemingly opposing emotions, by stating that Hashem is One. The attribute of mercy and the attribute of justice all come from the source*

---

6   *Pesachim* 50a.
7   *Devarim* 6:4.

of mercy. It is just **we** who perceive it as judgment and punishment. Even when you receive a "smack" from the Ribbono Shel Olam, when Hashem is strict and tough with you, it's also coming from the same source of mercy. Therefore, we can fear Hashem and love Him at the same time.

DAVID SINGS, NO MATTER WHAT

David HaMelech said, "Of kindness and judgment I sing."[8] The Gemara explains: "If I receive kindness from Hashem, I sing. If it's harsh judgment, I sing then too."[9]

The *Shaarei Teshuvah* tells us:[10]

When a person accepts the chastisement of Hashem and improves his ways and his deeds, he should be happy for the suffering he underwent because it helped him with very great and lofty benefits. He should thank Hashem, may He be blessed, for them just as he thanks Him for all other [types of] successes. As David HaMelech said, "I lift up the cup of salvation, and I call in the name of Hashem."[11] In another verse it says: "When I find distress and sorrow, I call in the name of Hashem."[12]

David's response was always the same. Nothing he received from Hakadosh Baruch Hu diminished his devotion even one iota.

In a complex incident, not to be taken at surface level, David HaMelech fathered a child from Batsheva. Be that as it may, David desperately wanted that child, who was sick from birth, to live. David prayed and fasted, refused to eat or wash himself, and was beside himself with anguish. When the child died, the *Tanach* says that David went to bathe, got dressed, and went to the place where the *Aron Kodesh* was in order

---

8   *Tehillim* 101:1.
9   *Berachos* 60b.
10 *Shaarei Teshuvah* 2:4.
11 *Tehillim* 116:13.
12 *Tehillim* 116:3–4.

to bow.¹³ The *Radak* says: "He went to thank Hashem for his *yissurim*." Not an easy thing to do. *Metzudes* adds: "This was in accordance with the rule that we must make a *berachah* on bad just as we do on good."

HAPPY WITH YISSURIM

The Sages taught us: "Those who have been embarrassed but do not embarrass others back, hear their disgrace but do not respond, serve [Hashem] from love and *are happy with their yissurim*—concerning such people the verse says, 'Those who love Him are likened to the sun when it comes out in all its might.'"¹⁴ All the aforementioned qualities are a sign of great might, including being happy when undergoing *yissurim*.

MY BUBBY

My mother, *a"h*, told me that when my Bubby was dying of cancer, she would daven and say, "Ribbono Shel Olam, I thank You for my suffering." My Bubby was a respected woman, but she was a simple Jew, relatively speaking. Throughout history, this was the attitude that our people always had.

I LOVE YOU EITHER WAY

This story was told to me by a close relative about her own grandmother. In the 1920s, her grandparents lived on the Lower East Side of New York and were renting an apartment for two dollars a month. They couldn't always come up with the two dollars because they were struggling to put bread on the table. One time, they fell two months behind in their rent. In those days, if the tenant was behind in the rent for two months, the law allowed the landlord to enter the apartment, empty out all the contents onto the street, and rent the apartment out to someone else. My relative's mother was a teenager at the time, and when she came home from school one day, she saw that all their possessions were out on the street. She sat down on the curb and started to cry. Her mother came home and said, "Chanie, why are you crying?"

---

13   *Shmuel II* 15–20.
14   *Gittin* 37b.

The daughter said, "Mama, don't you see? We don't have a roof over our heads!" She said, "Silly girl, for that you're crying?" And she lifted up her hands and said, "Ribbono Shel Olam, I love you with a roof over my head or without a roof over my head." This greatness was not uncommon among our grandmothers.

NOW I UNDERSTAND

In this life, on rare occasions we are given the gift of seeing the benefit of tough times. There is a verse that says: "And you will say on that day, 'I will thank You, Hashem, for You were wrought with me.'"[15] Why will we thank Hashem for having been angry with us, for having dealt harshly with us? This verse is talking about the time when the *galus* will finally come to an end, and we will experience the redemption through Mashiach. We have suffered so much in the long and bitter *galus* of almost two thousand years. Perhaps we have questions about why Hashem has done this to us. Therefore, the verse says that on that day it will be clear why it had to be this way, and that it was all for the good. Then we will thank Hashem for having been angry with us.

The Gemara compares this to a story of two people who were both trying to catch a ship.[16] They had business connections at the ship's destination and desperately needed to make it on time. One of them got a thorn in his foot, which slowed him down, and he came too late to catch the ship. He began to complain bitterly, "Hashem! How could You do this to me? You know how desperately I need this, and I haven't done anything to deserve this. Why did You do this to me?" After a few days passed, he heard that the ship had gone down at sea. He then began to praise Hakadosh Baruch Hu and thank Him for His kindness in making him miss that voyage.

We don't always get to see the benefits of what happens to us, even when the benefits are in this world. Certainly, we have no idea of the good that will accrue in the afterlife. Our task is to believe that

---

15 *Yeshayah* 12:1.
16 *Niddah* 31a.

everything that Hakadosh Baruch Hu does is ultimately for the good and that we don't truly know what is good for us.

A CHASSIDISHE STORY

Rav Simcha Wasserman used to tell the following story. When the Noam Elimelech was *niftar*, the Chassidim said that surely now their lot would improve because "*tzaddikim* are even greater after they die than they were during their lifetime."[17] *Tzaddikim* go up before the throne of glory and plead for their people. In Russia in those days, the persecution and the poverty were terrible, and there were many decrees against the Jews.

Unfortunately, things did *not* get better after their Rebbe's demise. Indeed, they became even worse. The Rebbe's *shamash* was very distraught, and he went to the Rebbe's grave. There he fell asleep, and the Rebbe appeared to him in a dream. He said, "I want you to know that when I was in this world, I used to pray to Hakadosh Baruch Hu to remove the *tzaros*. But now that I am in the world of truth, I find it hard to do that because I understand why the *tzaros* are needed."

JUST A LITTLE MORE

The Chafetz Chaim used to tell a *mashal*. There once was a Jew named Moishele, who lived under a *poritz* (the nobleman who owned the entire district). The Jew paid twenty rubles a year to rent his little plot of land. One time, the *poritz* announced that he would be taking a vacation. With travel the way it was in those days, it took very long to get from one country to another. When a nobleman took a vacation, it was for a long time. The *poritz* appointed a very cruel manager to oversee his properties in his absence. The instant the *poritz* departed, the manager came to Moishele and said, "Moishele, this year the rent is forty rubles, not twenty." Moishele said, "I can hardly manage to pay the twenty rubles; how am I going to be able to afford forty rubles?" The manager said, "I couldn't care less! I'm going to lash you once for every ruble you are short." When it came time to pay the rent, Moishele had only the

---

17   *Chullin* 7b.

twenty rubles. The manager told him in no uncertain terms, "Moishele, forty rubles." Moishele said, "I just couldn't manage the extra twenty." The manager had one of his strong workers force Moshe down, take off his shirt, and lash him viciously twenty times. Poor Moishele went home, broken in body and spirit. His wife, Zeldy, put some salve on Moishele's back, and he climbed into bed. Eventually, after quite some time, the wounds healed, but the scars were still there. Finally, the *poritz* returned home. Moishele ran to him and said, "My lord, I want to show you what your manager did." Moishele took off his shirt, turned around, showed him the scars and told him the story. The *poritz* was incensed. "What?! He did that to you? Call him in here!" The manager was summoned and had no choice but to admit his misdeed. Enraged, the *poritz* said, "For every lash you gave him, you're going to give him one acre of your land. Hand over twenty acres of your land to Moishele right now!" Moishele came home and told Zeldy what happened, and that now they were the rich landowners of twenty acres.

But then he started to cry. Zeldy asked, "You fool, what are you crying about now?" Moishele said, "Don't you understand? Isn't it a pity that he didn't lash me forty times? The pain of the lashes has already gone, and now we would have had forty acres instead of only twenty!"

The Chafetz Chaim says that when we get to *Olam Haba* and see how much we benefitted from the difficulties we went through in this world, we'll say, "Isn't it a pity that we didn't get a little bit more *yissurim* when we were living in the temporary life of *Olam Hazeh*."

ALWAYS GOOD

After the Bar Kochba revolution, the Romans were driven out of Eretz Yisrael, but they came back and reconquered one town at a time until they were about to take Yerushalayim as well. Bar Kochba and his men escaped to Beitar, which was a strongly fortified city. There was a siege that lasted three and a half years, and finally the Romans broke into the city. What followed was one of the greatest bloodbaths in history. About half a million people were killed in cold blood, as described at great length in the words of Chazal.

It is most likely that the numbers in the following statement are an exaggeration. However, the statement does indicate that there were vast numbers of young children learning Torah in Beitar.

> Rav Yehudah said in the name of Shmuel, in the name of Rabban Shimon ben Gamliel: What is meant by the verse, "My eye has caused me grief over all the daughters of my city"? There were four hundred shuls in the metropolis of Beitar, each one with four hundred Torah teachers. Each one had before him four hundred cheder children. When the enemy entered there, the children were stabbing them with their writing tools. When the enemy overpowered them and conquered them, they wrapped them in their sefarim and ignited them on fire.[18]

After the slaughter was over, the Roman emperor Adaryanus (Hadrian) did something very spiteful for revenge over the rebellion against him.

> Adaryanus owned a vineyard that was eighteen mil by eighteen mil, like the distance from Teverya to Tzipori.[19] He had the entire vineyard fenced with the dead bodies of the victims of Beitar, by standing the bodies upright and pressing them together, with their arms straight up in the air. They did not give off a foul smell and did not decay. It was decreed that they may not be buried, until another king arose and allowed them to be buried.[20]

In the course of all those years, the bodies had miraculously not decayed. The *Birkas Hamazon* we recite after eating bread originally had only three blessings. The fourth blessing was added at this point in history. The Gemara explains:

---

18 *Gittin* 58a.
19 A *mil* is two thousand *amos*, so the perimeter of his vineyard was as much as fifty-four miles around.
20 *Eichah Rabbah* 2:12.

> *The blessing of Ha'tov V'Ha'meitiv was instituted in Yavneh, concerning the ones who were murdered in Beitar. For Rav Masna said, the day that the harugei Beitar were finally buried, [the Sages] in Yavneh instituted [the blessing of] Ha'tov V'Ha'meitiv. "Ha'tov" [the good One], that they didn't decay, "V'Ha'meitiv" [and the One Who does good], that they were allowed to be buried.*[21]

What happened in Beitar was nothing short of a holocaust. At least some of the Sages in Yavneh had surely lost family, students, or friends there. Many people would become embittered after such a horrendous tragedy. Not the Jewish Sages. They authored a blessing in gratitude for the miracle and the ability to finally bury the dead: thanking Hashem for always being good to us, past, present, and future. No complaints, no doubts, no indignation. We see the good among the travails and give thanks to Hashem for always being good to us. This has always been the attitude of our people.

THE DARKNESS BRINGS THE LIGHT

Rabbeinu Yonah tells us:[22] "Even when a person is in the height of his distress, one who trusts Hashem should be hopeful that the darkness will be the cause of the ultimate light." As the verse says: "Don't rejoice, my enemy. When I fall, I'll get up. When I sit in darkness, Hashem is my light."[23] Chazal explain, "If I hadn't fallen, I wouldn't have been able to get up."[24] The falling was for the purpose of the getting up and for the ultimate rise in *hatzlachah*. "If I hadn't sat in the darkness, then I wouldn't have gotten the light." The *tzarah* was what I needed to bring the relief.

These concepts will not be absorbed from hearing a lecture or from just reading a book. It can take a lifetime of contemplation to internalize fully these *hashkafah* concepts. As we stated earlier, it is easy to

---

21 *Berachos* 48b.
22 *Shaarei Teshuvah* 2:5.
23 *Michah* 7:8.
24 *Midrash Tehillim* 22.

say these thoughts, but it is very hard to internalize them emotionally. Nevertheless, it is incumbent upon us to at least understand these ideas with our intellect, even if we have not yet internalized them with our emotions. And so, we continue.

WE DON'T ASK FOR YISSURIM

In truth, we never ask Hakadosh Baruch Hu to give us suffering, even when it's for our good. Although we believe that everything that happens to us is for our good, we still daven that *yissurim* should not come on us. *Yissurim* are a very big test for a person, and we are afraid to be tested. We certainly don't want to have to endure the pain. Therefore, we ask Hashem to help us achieve what the *yissurim* are intended to accomplish without having to undergo them.

A person who has a serious illness and has to take very bitter medicine is grateful that he has the medicine he needs. Still, he would greatly prefer not to have needed that medicine. We, too, hope that through the merit of our *tefillos* we will be able to be "healed"—without the *yissurim*. But if the *yissurim* have been decreed upon us, then we have no choice but to accept them, while continuing to ask Hashem for mercy. We do ours and Hakadosh Baruch Hu does His. And when He does His, we submit to His will.

Nevertheless, when distress does come on us, we have to realize that despite first appearances, it's a very big favor. All the suffering of Iyov is not comparable to one second in Gehinnom. Therefore, it is a great benefit when a person gets his suffering in this world. Although a person would never willingly choose such a thing, nevertheless, it is a favor when it does happen.

HOW TERRIBLE AN AVEIRAH IS

How great our need for atonement is when we do an *aveirah*. We have to remember that a sin is compared to the stars. Just as the stars look merely like little dots in the sky, truthfully many of them are many times greater than our sun. So, too, we don't realize the severity of a sin. It looks very small to us, seemingly no big deal. We don't realize the *churban*, the destruction that we cause when we do an *aveirah*.

When a child is on a train and pulls the brightly colored emergency cord, making the train stop, everyone is screaming at him. He has no idea what he did wrong and what everyone wants from him. All he did was pull on a colored cord. Perhaps when we commit an *aveirah*, we also don't appreciate the severity of what we have done. The simple person doesn't know why he shouldn't stand on a wet floor when he's changing a fuse. All he knows is that it says in his how-to book that when you change a fuse, don't stand on a wet floor. He may not understand the principle, but he follows what it says in the booklet without understanding. If he doesn't comply, he will be sorry. We have our Torah, our instruction booklet, to tell us what is good for us, what's bad for us, what's healthy, and what's poisonous. We comply with full trust in the Heavenly author of our manual.

THE INSTALLMENT PLAN

Hakadosh Baruch Hu accepts payment from us on an installment plan. Every little discomfort is recorded in our account. If someone sticks his hand in his pocket to pull out a quarter and accidentally pulls out a nickel, it is just a small annoyance.[25] Nevertheless, Hakadosh Baruch Hu subtracts it from the *yissurim* that are supposed to come on him.

> # Summing Up
> Bitter medicine is not pleasant to take. Nevertheless, when we need it, the doctor is doing us a favor in prescribing it. So, too, when hard times come, they need to be viewed as bitter but necessary.

---

25 *Arachin* 16b.

CHAPTER
ELEVEN

The Mystery of Gehinnom

One of the most perturbing and frightening aspects of the Torah faith is the concept of Gehinnom. Why would Hashem put someone through such distress and pain? Perhaps we can shed a little light on the matter and dispel some of the negative feelings associated with Gehinnom.

THANKS FOR GEHINNOM

Chazal tell us something quite astounding, based on the explanation of a verse: The wicked in Gehinnom are actually grateful for what they undergo in Gehinnom.

Rabbi Yehoshua ben Levi said:

> What is the meaning of the verse, "Those who pass over the valley of crying transform it into a fountain; also they enwrap their guide with blessings"?[1]
>
> "They pass over" means they transgressed the will of Hakadosh Baruch Hu. "The valley" means that they are in a deep place in Gehinnom. "Of crying" means that they cry and shed tears like

---

[1] Tehillim 84:7.

the fountain of Shetin. "They enwrap their guide with blessings" means that they justify their judgment on themselves and say before Him, "Master of the World, You judged well. You declared meritorious well [for the righteous]. You declared guilty well [for the wicked]. You did well in creating Gehinnom for the wicked and Gan Eden for the righteous."[2]

There they realize that Gehinnom is a cleansing process designed for their benefit, which will prepare them to eventually enter Gan Eden.

A CLEANSING FOR ETERNITY

Imagine a person who is friendly with the emperor and has an appointment to visit him in his throne room. While on the way, dressed in his finest clothing, he slips and falls into a mud hole. Now he is caked with mud from head to toe. His cell phone rings, and it's the emperor on the phone. The emperor tells him that it's perfectly alright for him to come just as he is. What will his response be? "Your majesty! Please let me go home, clean myself, and change my clothes. I wouldn't want to enter the palace in this condition."

Precisely the same way, when the *neshamah* leaves this world, it is headed for a meeting with Hashem. But *aveiros* dirty the *neshamah*, and the person would never want to appear before Hashem all soiled. Therefore, Gehinnom has been prepared as a place where the *neshamah* gets cleansed and can then enter the palace in purity and cleanliness.

IT WAS ALL WORTH IT

Rabbi Itzele Peterburger, an esteemed *talmid* of Rabbi Yisrael Salanter, shares an astounding thought.[3] The Gemara relates a story about the only sage among the Tanna'im who became a heretic: Elisha ben Avuya.[4] Most people will recognize him by his nickname "Acher." Originally, he was Rabbi Meir's first *rebbi*, but he subsequently became an enemy of the Jewish People. The Gemara offers various causes that

---

2 *Eruvin* 19a.
3 *Ohr Yisrael*, p. 127.
4 *Chagigah* 15b.

made him leave the path of Torah. Whatever the cause for his defection, he became a true *rasha* and a traitor, despite being a tremendous *talmid chacham*. Rabbi Meir tried all his life to get Acher to do *teshuvah* without success, so he died a *rasha*. The Sages saw with their *ruach hakodesh* that after Acher's death, he was in no man's land. He definitely couldn't get into Gan Eden because he had sinned so excessively, but he also wasn't allowed into Gehinnom either. Could someone who learned so much Torah burn in Gehinnom?

Because of this, Acher's *neshamah* was in limbo. Rabbi Meir said, "If I am *chashuv* in the other world, when I die, smoke will come out of Acher's grave." That would be a sign that Acher had been accepted into Gehinnom. When Rabbi Meir died, smoke began coming out of Acher's grave. Much later, Rabbi Yochanan said, "Is that a work of strength, to burn his *rebbi* in Gehinnom? If I am considered worthy in the other world, I am going to ask them to finally take him into Gan Eden." When Rabbi Yochanan died, the smoke stopped coming out of Acher's grave, a sign that he had finally been accepted into Gan Eden.

Rav Itzele Peterburger calculates for us that from the death of Rabbi Meir to the death of Rabbi Yochanan was approximately one hundred and fifty years! Rabbi Meir didn't know how long Acher would have to burn in Gehinnom. He could have remained even longer in Gehinnom if Rabbi Yochanan had not come along to get him out. Rabbi Meir knew that no matter how long Acher would remain in Gehinnom, it would be worth it for him, because when he would finally be released, his rectification complete and his soul cleansed, he could go to Gan Eden forever and enjoy the great reward for the Torah that he learned and the mitzvos he originally did.

A GREAT FAVOR

The Gemara tells a story about a sage named Avdan, a student of Rabbeinu HaKadosh. The *talmidim* were waiting for Rebbi to come start the *shiur*. The *talmidim* used to sit on the floor, while Rebbi would sit on a chair. When Rebbi arrived, everyone went to their places to sit down. Rabbi Yishmael ben Rabbi Yosi was a great scholar, but was very heavy and moved slowly. By the time everyone else had already taken their places, he was still winding his way through the crowd that was already sitting, stepping over them to get to his place. Avdan said to him, "Who is this that is stepping over the heads of the holy people?" In other words, what are you doing climbing through the crowd? A back-and-forth discussion ensued, and Rebbi began the *shiur*. Meanwhile, a question came to Rebbi, who needed some information before he could respond. He sent Avdan to go and check into the matter so he would know how to answer the question. After Avdan left, Rabbi Yishmael arose and said, "My father, Rabbi Yosi, already answered this question." Once he told Rebbi the answer, Rebbi called Avdan back. He told Avdan that he didn't need the information anymore because this great sage, Rabbi Yishmael ben Rabbi Yosi, had already provided the needed answer. Now Avdan needed to return to his place, so he started climbing over everyone, just as Rabbi Yishmael had done before, and for which Avdan had publicly rebuked him. Rabbi Yishmael ben Rabbi Yosi said, "Someone whom the *am kadosh* needs has a right to climb over the *am kodesh*, but someone like you who is not needed, what right do you have to climb over the *am kadosh*?" He meant to say, you rebuked me for exactly the same thing you just did. Rebbi then told Avdan, "Stay at the end of the crowd; don't climb over everybody."

The Gemara quotes a *Beraisa*: "At that time, Avdan contracted *tzaraas* [leprosy], his two sons drowned, and his two daughters-in-law separated from their husbands." Rav Nachman bar Yitzchak said, "Blessed is Hashem Who punished Avdan in this world and not in the World to Come." He meant to say, "What a big favor Hashem did for him, that he punished him in this world!" This was seemingly not a major sin, but nevertheless, Avdan received some very severe punishments for it. He would never have wished these punishments on himself, nor would anyone wish them on him. But when the punishments came, Rav Nachman bar Yitzchak said, "Blessed is Hashem Who punished Avdan in this world rather than in the next."[5]

---

5   *Yevamos* 105b.

I remember vividly hearing this Gemara quoted by the saintly Rav Yechezkel Levenstein. As stated, we never ask for *yissurim*, but they are a great favor compared to the alternative in the afterlife.

WE WOULDN'T STAND A CHANCE

The Vilna Gaon says an amazing thing in *Even Sheleimah*: "If not for the suffering that we undergo, we wouldn't find our hands and feet in *Olam Haba*." That expression means we wouldn't stand a chance. We have to get cleansed before we enter the palace.

WHAT DO YOU KNOW, MY CHILD?

Why can't it be different, though? If we were able to ask Hakadosh Baruch Hu, "Why does it have to be this way?" He would undoubtedly say, "My child, what do you know about eternity? What do you know about the *neshamah*? What do you know about the severity of a sin, the appropriate punishment, and the need for atonement? You're not able to understand right now, but that's the way it has to be. I understand better."

Sometimes what looks like a little mole is really a tumor, but the layman doesn't know it. He goes to the doctor, who can tell what it really is. When the *neshamah* separates from the body, then things will become clearer, and the *neshamah* will understand much more.

> ## Summing Up
> Even Gehinnom is a favor for those who need it.
> We cannot appreciate it during our lifetime, but those in Gehinnom perceive it as positive.

CHAPTER TWELVE

Yissurim and Tzaddikim

There are other possible reasons that a person sometimes goes through difficulties in this world, in addition to those already stated. Many such reasons have been revealed to us in our Torah.

THE DEATH OF TZADDIKIM

"The death of *tzaddikim* atones" for the generation, as it says: "Why is the death of Miriam written immediately after the portion of *parah adumah*? To tell us that 'just as sacrifices atone, the death of *tzaddikim* also atones.'"[1] Sometimes Hakadosh Baruch Hu takes a *tzaddik* away from the world to bring atonement for the sins of that generation. The *tzaddik* devotes his entire life to being *kodesh l'Hashem* and to being totally devoted to the needs of Klal Yisrael. He gives up many comforts, sometimes even living in poverty, because he neglects his own livelihood to be constantly focused on doing for his people. For this, he will receive tremendous reward in *Olam Haba*. Similarly, sometimes Hakadosh Baruch Hu asks of the *tzaddik* that he should forgo his life

---

1 *Moed Katan* 28a.

altogether for the sake of a being a *korban* for the *dor*. For this, too, he will be amply recompensed in *Olam Haba*.

THROUGH MY CLOSEST ONES

When Nadav and Avihu died, Moshe Rabbeinu said to Aharon, "That is what Hashem spoke: 'With my closest ones I will be sanctified, and in front of the entire people, I will be honored.' Aharon remained silent."[2] *Rashi* quotes from Chazal: "Moshe said to Aharon, 'Aharon, my brother! I knew that this house would be sanctified by the beloved ones of the Omnipresent. I thought that it would be either me or you, but now I see that they are greater than I and you.'"[3] Moshe knew—from a hint in Hashem's words—that through a punishment that would come upon His very closest ones, the people would realize the severity and the strictness of the *Mishkan* and would know to treat it with the proper respect and reverence. It was Nadav and Avihu who were chosen to make this sacrifice—to give up their lives so that Klal Yisrael would learn to have reverence for the *Mishkan*.

HOW CHASHUV YOU ARE

The Gemara tells us an amazing story.[4] Rav Chiya bar Abba was a *rebbi* of one of Reish Lakish's sons. A son of Rav Chiya bar Abba died. There are two versions in the Gemara regarding the age of the deceased child and exactly what Reish Lakish told Rav Chiya. According to one version, the son who died was a young child, and Reish Lakish quoted a verse in *Ha'azinu*: "Hashem saw, and He became angry from the anger of His sons and daughters."[5] Reish Lakish explained this to mean that "in a generation that the fathers anger Hakadosh Baruch Hu, He gets angry at their children, their sons and daughters, and they die when they're young."

The second version is that the child was already a *bachur*, and Reish Lakish quoted a verse in *Yeshayah*, which states that in a generation

---

2   *Vayikra* 10:3.
3   *Vayikra Rabbah* 12:2.
4   *Kesubos* 8b.
5   *Devarim* 32:19.

where the people speak dirty language (*nivul peh*): "Hashem will not rejoice over His young men and will not have mercy on His widows and His orphans because they are all doing bad things, and every mouth is speaking dirty language."[6]

The Gemara asks the following. Reish Lakish came to be *menachem avel* but spoke to Rav Chiya with such harshness, saying that his child died because of his punishments! How could Reish Lakish act this way?

The Gemara answers: "This is what he said [in order] to convey: "*Chashuv at*—You are a very highly thought of person [in Heaven] to be held responsible for the sins of the generation." In other words, you were chosen to bring a *korban* for the sins of the generation.

A KORBAN FOR THE GENERATION

When I was first married, a tragedy befell a family with whom I was very friendly. On the way home from buying a hat for his bar mitzvah, their son was hit by a truck and died on Erev Shabbos. The *levayah* was on Sunday. It was, as you can imagine, a highly emotional funeral. Rav Moshe Feinstein did not know the family, but he heard about the tragedy and came to speak at the *levayah*. I was present and have never forgotten what he said:

> It is true that sometimes young children are taken for the sins of their parents. But these parents are chashuve b'nei Torah, and there is absolutely no reason to think that is the case. As far as his own sins, the child was still a katan and has no responsibility for whatever sins he may have committed. We have to say that Hakadosh Baruch Hu took a korban for this dor, to be mechaper for the sins of this generation.

The *tzaddik* never loses out as a result of this. If we could now go to visit those children or *tzaddikim* who were taken away as an atonement for the *dor* and we were to ask them, "Do you have any regrets?" they would say, "No! I've been paid overtime, with bonuses, here in Olam Haba."

---

6   *Yeshayah* 9:16.

PLUCKED AWAY WHILE STILL GOOD

Sometimes a *tzaddik* is removed from this world as a favor to him because he is beginning to succumb to the temptation to sin. Hakadosh Baruch Hu therefore plucks him out of the world in advance so that he can arrive in the afterlife as a *zakai* (pure person).

Chanoch is listed in the genealogy of the ten generations from Adam until Noach. He lived hundreds of years less than anyone else mentioned there. The verse says that "Chanoch walked with Hashem, and he is no longer, for Hashem took him away."[7] *Rashi* explains that the unusual expression "he is not here" means "in the world to fill up his [allotted] years." "He was a *tzaddik*, but it was easy in his mind to turn into a *rasha*. Therefore, Hashem hurried up to remove him." There was a lot of pressure on Chanoch, as well as negative environmental influences, and he was weakening. Hakadosh Baruch Hu did him a big favor. Instead of letting Chanoch stay around longer and deteriorate, He removed him from this world hundreds of years early.

LONGER LASTING FOR THE JOURNEY

> When Rabbi Yochanan would reach the following verse, he would cry. "'Behold! In His holy ones He does not trust.'[8] If He does not trust in His holy ones, in whom does He trust?" One day, he was walking on the road and saw someone picking figs. He left the ripe ones and took the figs that were not ripe. He said to him, "Aren't these better than those?" The person answered, "I need these for a trip. The unripened ones will last, but the ripe ones won't." Rabbi Yochanan said, "That is the meaning of the verse, 'Behold! In His holy ones He does not trust.'"[9]

Rashi explains: "He is afraid that the good ones will rot. Righteous young men, too, are [sometimes] put to death [early] lest they sin."

---

7   *Bereishis* 5:22–24.
8   *Iyov* 15:15.
9   *Chagigah* 5a.

YISSURIM OF LOVE

There is another cause of suffering called *"yissurin shel ahavah—* affliction that comes from love." This is a difficult concept for the average person to relate to, but we must try to wrap our heads around it since Chazal have told us about it, and they derive it from *Tanach*. Rashi tells us that these *yissurim* are given for no sin at all, but only to increase the reward of the *tzaddik* in *Olam Haba*. The harder it is to keep mitzvos and to serve Hashem, the more reward he will get. Therefore, sometimes, Hakadosh Baruch Hu afflicts certain great *tzaddikim* in this world so that they will get an infinitely greater share in *Olam Haba*. "Rava said in the name of Rav Schora, in the name of Rav Huna, 'Anyone whom Hakadosh Baruch Hu really loves, He crushes them with *yissurim*.'"[10] The Gemara applies this principle to the tragic story of Rabbi Yochanan, whose ten sons all died.

Rabbi Yochanan took a tooth from his last son, and when he encountered people whose losses and travails made them embittered, he would say, "This is the bone of my tenth child [who died]."[11] He meant that just as he continued to move on in life, so too must those who have suffered move on and overcome their grief.

This was *yissurin shel ahavah*. For people who are not one hundred percent focused on *Olam Haba*, this is incomprehensible. For *tzaddikim* such as Rabbi Yochanan, who have the spiritual strength to bear the *yissurim* and continue their lives with full productivity, the suffering is ultimately more than worthwhile and is even a sign of Hashem's love for them.

Summing Up

Now we have learned some additional possible reasons why a person may be taken away "early" or given *yissurim*:

- As a *korban* for the generation, for which the *tzaddik* will be amply reimbursed in *Olam Haba*.
- To take him away before he spoils.
- *Yissurim shel ahavah* for the very great *tzaddikim*.

---

10   *Berachos* 5a.
11   *Rashbam, Bava Basra* 116a.

CHAPTER THIRTEEN

Responsibility for Others

Among the many reasons that a good person may undergo suffering is for negligence in fulfilling the mitzvah of giving rebuke. Even a meritorious person, an *ehrlicher Yid*, can be punished for a sin that he himself never committed because he did not rebuke someone else who transgressed that sin.

ALL JEWS ARE RESPONSIBLE FOR ONE ANOTHER

When the Torah warns us about the consequences of forsaking the mitzvos, it says: "They will stumble, each one over his brother."[1] Besides the simple meaning of running away in haste and tripping over one another, Chazal also infer that "each one will stumble over the sins of his brother."[2] This teaches that all of Yisrael are responsible for each other. Each and every Jew will be liable for the sins of his fellow Jew. Therefore, if one person does a sin, the other person will be held responsible for him if he could have rebuked him and prevented him from doing so.

I heard a *mashal* long ago that illustrates this idea. People rented seats on a boat. As they were traveling, one person took out a drill

---
1 *Vayikra* 26:37.
2 *Sanhedrin* 27b.

and started drilling a hole under his seat. The person next to him said, "What in the world are you doing?" The man with the drill answered, "What is it your business? I paid for my seat; I can do whatever I want!" His neighbor said, "It is my business! If you make a hole under your seat, we all drown!" So too, if someone does an *aveirah*, it's everyone's business because they may have to pay the price for it.

DON'T BEAR THE SIN

The Torah says: "Rebuke your friend, and don't bear a sin because of him."[3] What does "don't bear a sin because of him" mean?

- *Rashi* says it means you shouldn't rebuke him in public. Go to him privately, take him aside, and tell him nicely, but if you rebuke him in public, you will get a sin instead of a mitzvah.
- *Ramban* says it means you should rebuke him when he sins, or else you will carry away his sin, and it will be considered as if you did that sin yourself.

Perhaps one of the reasons we say *viduy* on Yom Kippur for sins that we may have never personally committed is that we may be responsible for not rebuking someone else who did.

HIS NEIGHBOR'S COW

A person may not allow his animal to do a forbidden work on Shabbos. It states explicitly in the Ten Commandments: "And the seventh day is a Shabbos to Hashem, your G-d. Do not do any *melachah*, you, your son and daughter, your slave and maidservant, and your animal, and your convert in your cities."[4]

For example, you cannot place a package on your cow and send it across a public domain (*reshus ha'rabim*) because the cow will be carrying for you. When a person wears something that makes them look nice on Shabbos, it is not considered to be included in the *melachah* of carrying, as it is considered as part of their clothing. But if he puts a ribbon between a cow's horns, although people might think it looks pretty,

---

3   *Vayikra* 19:17.
4   *Shemos* 20:10.

it doesn't do anything for the cow. The ribbon is therefore considered a burden, and the cow is performing a *melachah* by carrying the ribbon for him across the *reshus ha'rabim*. He has transgressed the prohibition against working one's animal on Shabbos.

The Mishnah records something quite astounding: "Rabbi Elazar ben Azariah's cow went out with a ribbon between its horns, against the will of the *chachamim*."[5]

Rabbi Elazar ben Azariah, the Nasi of Yisrael, one of the greatest sages of all time, was guilty of allowing his cow to go out in a public place on Shabbos with a ribbon between its horns? This is a transgression of a Torah law!

The Gemara asks there: "Rabbi Elazar ben Azariah's cow? Did he have only one cow? Didn't Rav Yehudah say, in the name of Rav, that Rabbi Elazar ben Azariah used to give twelve thousand animals every year for *maaser*?" He was a very wealthy man with lots of cows. The Mishnah should have said: "One of Rabbi Elazar ben Azariah's cows," or, "All of Rabbi Elazar ben Azariah's cows," but not, "Rabbi Elazar ben Azariah's cow," as if he had only one cow. The Gemara answers: "It was not his cow at all. It was actually his neighbor's cow, but because he didn't rebuke the neighbor, the sin is accredited to him."

The Mishnah was written the way the matter is perceived in the world of truth. In *olam ha'emes*, had Rabbi Elazar ben Azariah arrived there without having done *teshuvah* (which he did), he would have been confronted by the Heavenly court. They would have said, "You transgressed the *aveirah* of *shevisas beheimah* on Shabbos." He would surely have responded, "Me? In my entire life, I never did such a thing." They would have said, "Yes, you never did so personally, but your neighbor's cow went out with a ribbon between its horns. You saw it from the corner of your eye, but you were too busy being the Nasi of the Jewish People. You didn't stop to rebuke your neighbor; therefore, the sin is accredited to your account."

---

5   *Shabbos* 54b.

RESPONSIBLE FOR WHOEVER WILL LISTEN

We see from Chazal that whoever has the ability to rebuke and doesn't do so is held responsible for that sin. The Gemara continues with some very frightening statements here:

> Rav and Rabbi Chanina, Rabbi Yochanan and Rav Chaviva made the following statement: "Whoever has the ability to protest to the members of his household [his family] is held responsible for the sins of the members of his household. [If he is able to rebuke] the people of his city, he is held responsible for the sins of his city. [If he could rebuke] the whole world, he is held responsible for the entire world." Rav Papa said, "The people in the house of the Reish Galusa [head of the exiles] are held responsible for the whole world."[6]

Let's think about this:

- If someone's spouse or children are committing a sin that he could correct by rebuking them but he neglects to do so, he is held guilty for their sins.
- An individual who is respected in his city and could take a stand on something the people of the city are doing wrong is held responsible for all the *aveiros* of the city.
- There are individuals who are so influential that everyone in the Jewish world would listen to them. Such a person has to speak up and protest against the sins of his generation. If he doesn't, he has all the sins of the generation on his head.
- In Bavel, which was the main center of Torah for many hundreds of years, there was a descendant of the house of David who was appointed by the Babylonian government to oversee the internal affairs of the Jewish People. Hence, he was entitled *Reish Galusa*, the "head of the exiles." He had the authority and power of a ruler, with a police force, and his word was law. Rav Papa therefore said that if the *Reish Galusa* did not rebuke the people

---

6   *Shabbos* 54b.

and enforce the laws of Torah, he would be held responsible for all the sins of the [Jewish] world.

The Gemara continues:

> *This is in accordance with what Rabbi Chanina said: "What is the meaning of the verse, 'Hashem will come in judgment on the elders of His people and His ministers?'[7] If the ministers sinned, did the elders sin? [The elders were the tzaddikim, whereas the ministers were the corrupt members of the government. The answer is that it means:] The elders will be taken into judgment because they didn't protest against the ministers."*

The Gemara continues with another story. Rav Yehudah was sitting in front of his *rebbi*, Shmuel, and learning. A certain woman came along and complained that she had some kind of a court case, but no one was paying attention to her. Shmuel paid no heed to her. Rav Yehudah said to his *rebbi*, "Doesn't the *Rebbi* consider what it says in the verse: 'One who closes his ears to the outcry of the poor man, he too shall call out and not be answered'?"[8] (In other words, why are you ignoring this lady who is coming to you with a complaint?) Shmuel said, "You smart one, your *rebbi* is in cold water. Your *rebbi*'s *rebbi* [who is his superior] is in hot water. Mar Ukva is the head of the *beis din*." He meant that since Mar Ukva was present there, it was his responsibility to take care of it. "It has nothing to do with me. I don't have to worry about this."

Shmuel thought that was the end of it, but we will soon see otherwise.

The Gemara tells us a story: "Rav Yosef the son of Rav Yehoshua fainted and died."[9] He had what we would call an out-of-body experience, and he came back. "His father said to him, 'What did you see?' He said to him, 'I saw an upside-down world. The ones who are on top [here] were on the bottom [there], and the ones who are on the bottom [here] were on the top [there].'"

---

7   *Yeshayah* 3:14.
8   *Mishlei* 21:13.
9   *Bava Basra* 10b.

Rashi explains: "The ones who are highest here because of their wealth [i.e., arrogant people who ignore the poor] were on the bottom, and I saw the poor people, who are considered low among us, very respected there. They were on the top." Rav Yehoshua said to Rav Yosef that actually, "What you saw was the clear world." He meant that that is not an upside-down world at all.

Tosafos brings an astonishing quotation here:

> *Rabbeinu Chananel explains that the Geonim said they had a tradition, one Rav from another Rav, that what Rav Yosef the son of Rav Yehoshua saw was Shmuel sitting in front of Rav Yehudah. Rav Yehudah had protested against Shmuel in the case of the woman who came and complained before Shmuel, but Shmuel paid no attention. Rav Yehudah asked why he didn't take into account the verse that says, "One who ignores the outcry of the poor man will also cry out and not be answered."*[10]

The period of the Geonim wasn't so long after this incident with Rav Yosef the son of Rav Yehoshua happened. The Geonim had passed down this information in an unbroken chain from that time. Although in this world, Rav Yehudah was the *talmid* and Shmuel was the *rebbi*, in the other world, it was the opposite. This was all because Rav Yehudah was correct that Shmuel was supposed to have taken care of that woman—whether by speaking to the people who were afflicting her or arranging that the court should look after her—but he neglected to do so. Therefore, in heaven he was punished by being the *talmid* instead of the *rebbi*.

EVEN IF THEY WON'T LISTEN

The Gemara brings another very frightening story.

> *Rabbi Zeira said to Rabbi Simon, "Why don't you rebuke the people of the Reish Galusa? These people who are in charge are*

---

10   *Bava Basra* 10b.

doing a lot of wrong things, and you should rebuke them." Rabbi Simon said, "They won't accept rebuke from me." Rabbi Zeira said, "Even though they won't accept your rebuke, you should rebuke them anyway." Rabbi Acha ben Rabbi Chanina said, "There was never a good promise that came from Hakadosh Baruch Hu that He took back, except for one. As it is written: Hashem said to him [the angel], 'Pass through the city of Yerushalayim and inscribe the letter tav on the foreheads of the people who moan and groan about all of the abominations that are being done in Yerushalayim.' Hakadosh Baruch Hu said to Gavriel, 'Go and mark the letter tav in ink on the foreheads of tzaddikim so that the angels of destruction shall not have power over them. On the foreheads of the resha'im, mark the letter tav in blood so that the angels of destruction will have power over them.' The attribute of justice said, 'Ribbono Shel Olam! What is the difference between these and those?' [Hashem] responded, 'These are complete tzaddikim, and those are complete resha'im.' [The attribute of justice] said, 'They should have rebuked, but they did not!' He said back, 'It is revealed and known before Me that if they had rebuked them, they never would have accepted it.' [The attribute of justice] said, 'If it was revealed before you, was it revealed before them?' That is the meaning of what is written 'elders, young men and girls, children and women kill destructively, but on every person that has the [letter] tav on him, do not approach. [That was what Hashem said originally. Then He retracted and said,] 'From My holiest ones you shall start.'"[11]

We see that at the time of the *churban* of Yerushalayim and the First Beis Hamikdash, the *tzaddikim* were not spared because they didn't rebuke the wicked sufficiently.

---

11   *Shabbos* 55a.

Summing Up

Many times, *yissurim* come for sins that people have committed. If we see a truly righteous person suffering, it may be because sins are being added to his account due to failure to rebuke or forewarn others who might have listened.

A person may be held responsible for sins he never committed if he had the opportunity to rebuke others or use his authority to make them desist from the sin. From all the above citations, we see how great this responsibility is and how severely a person can be punished for neglecting to rebuke. When we see the good person going through *yissurim*, it may be that he is being afflicted for someone else's sins.

CHAPTER
FOURTEEN

A Deeper Glimpse into Divine Providence

There is another very noteworthy concept that sometimes comes into the picture. Hakadosh Baruch Hu is more particular with the mistakes and the sins of the *tzaddikim* than He is with the shortcomings of plain people: "He is exacting with His most pious ones to a hairsbreadth."[1]

The following story will serve to illustrate this. Rav Elya Lopian grew up in Lithuania, and his mother used to raise chickens in their yard, as was common practice. Once, when he was a little boy, he was running around the house a bit wildly, knocked a glass off the table, and it broke. His mother gave him a little slap and told him to stop running around so wild. A few minutes later, one of the chickens flew into the house, flew around the table, and knocked a glass off the table, which fell and broke. Little Elya assumed the chicken would get a slap for breaking a glass, just as he had a few minutes before. His mother took the chicken

---

1   *Bava Kama* 50a.

by the wings and shooed it out of the house without as much as a single slap. Elya said, "It's not fair! When I break a glass, I get a smack. When the chicken breaks a glass, it gets nothing! I would rather be a chicken!"

Rav Elya said that when he got a little older, he came to understand that although a human being has to pay more serious consequences for his actions than a chicken, it's still preferable to be a human being than a chicken.

It is true that the *tzaddik* is more answerable for his mistakes than a plain person. But that doesn't mean it isn't worth it to be a *tzaddik* because, in the final analysis, his ultimate reward will be worth the consequences he endured.

RIGHT IN FRONT OF THE KING

If someone commits a minor crime out in the street, such as a parking offense or some other minor misdemeanour, a fine is a fair punishment. But when one stands in front of the king in the throne room, even a minor offense is considered a major crime. The great *tzaddikim* live constantly with the awareness that they stand directly before Hakadosh Baruch Hu. They are in his "throne room," so to speak. Therefore, what is expected of them is much greater than what is expected of simple people.

Moshe Rabbeinu was told by Hashem to go to Mitzrayim and redeem the Jewish People. His younger son Eliezer had just recently been born. When he got to Mitzrayim, the Torah states: "It was when he was in a hotel, Hashem met up with him, and wanted to kill him."[2] Chazal explain that an angel came and swallowed Moshe up from his head down to the place of the *bris*, and from his feet up until that place. Moshe's wife, Tzipporah, understood that this was a hint of punishment for not yet having circumcised Eliezer, so she herself gave him a *bris milah*. Then the angel let Moshe Rabbeinu go. Chazal initially explained that Moshe had been lax in performing a *bris*, and that was why he was punished. "Rabbi Yosi said, '*Chas v'shalom*! That great *tzaddik* Moshe Rabbeinu

---

2   *Shemos* 4:24.

was not lax."³ This is what happened: When he was commanded to go to Mitzrayim, he said, "If I make the *bris* before I leave, then it is a danger to travel with the child for three days. I have no choice. I'll have to delay the *bris*." So why then was he punished? Because when he came to Egypt, "he first got busy finding a hotel room." He should have made the *bris* wherever he stopped. But because he wasted a few minutes looking for a more suitable place to make the *bris*, for him that was considered a major delay. It was as if Hakadosh Baruch Hu was standing over him saying, "Nu, make the *bris* already!" and still he delayed. For us it wouldn't have been considered an offense, but for Moshe Rabbeinu it was considered a major crime.

STRICT WITH HIS MOST PIOUS ONES

The Gemara relates that there was a person named Nechunya, "the digger of pits."⁴ He used to dig water pits for the people coming up to Yerushalayim for Yom Tov so they would have water to drink. One time, a daughter of his fell into one of the pits. They came and informed Rabbi Chanina ben Dosa. Although this was just before the destruction of the Second Beis Hamikdash, which was not a time of open miracles, Rabbi Chanina ben Dosa was accustomed to having miracles happen to him because of his extreme piety.

Therefore, when Rabi Chanina ben Dosa was informed for the first time about the incident, he answered, "Shalom."

They came back a little while later, and again he said, "Shalom." The third time they came back, he said, "She's out already."

When they saw the daughter, they asked, "Who brought you out of the pit?" She said, "There was a male sheep that was being led by an old man." (Avraham Avinu came to take her out.)

They came back to Chanina ben Dosa and said, "You are a *navi*, you knew she was out." He said, "I'm not a *navi*, and I'm not the son of a *navi*, but I said to myself, is it possible that one of his own children

---

3   *Nedarim* 31b.
4   *Bava Kama* 50a.

would die in the water pits that this *tzaddik* had pained himself to dig for others? It couldn't be, so I knew that she would be saved."

The Gemara says, nevertheless, that a son of Nechunya's died of thirst. We don't know what the circumstances of this were because the Gemara doesn't tell us. Yet, "Hakadosh Baruch Hu is exacting with His pious ones to a hair's breadth." In the exact thing that Nechunya put in so much effort, the water pits, he could not be harmed. But in some other way, he could.

> ## Summing Up
> A relatively minor sin done by a *tzaddik* is far more serious than if it would have been done by the average person. The *tzaddik* should know better and is viewed in Heaven as if he stands right before the King in His palace.

CHAPTER FIFTEEN

Gilgul

We have already offered a number of reasons why a *tzaddik* might sometimes suffer in this world, but ultimately it will benefit him in the afterlife. There is another explanation of "*tzaddik v'ra lo*" that will open a window for us to realize how little we understand about how Hashem operates.

There is a concept brought many, many times in numerous classic *sefarim* that a *neshamah* that did not fulfill its purpose when it was in this world may be sent down again, in the body of another person, to find what is called its *tikkun*, "correction." When the person finally fulfills his purpose, the *neshamah* will have earned its just rewards in Gan Eden. Therefore, when we see a *tzaddik* suffering, it may not be due to anything that he has done in this life, but rather for something that "he"—that is, his *neshamah*—did before, in his previous existence.

It is not unfair to hold a person responsible now for what he did last time around. If we have internalized the idea that the essence of the person is not the body, but the *neshamah*, and that the body is merely a garment for the *neshamah*, then it is not a question of making one person suffer for what a "different" person did. It's not a different person at all, but rather the same person, just in a new set of clothing. When someone who has a debt changes his clothes, he is no less responsible to pay than while wearing the clothing in which he incurred the debt. In our case, even though the person does not know why he's being punished or why he must undergo these travails, the *neshamah* certainly remembers and understands, and it's the *neshamah* that needs to know.

The Chafetz Chaim used to say, "Once we take into account the possibility of *gilgul*, reincarnation, it is really quite impossible to ask any questions at all about how Hakadosh Baruch Hu conducts the world." After all, how do we know what the person did last time around? The concept of *gilgul* reminds us how little we know. Who knows how many other spiritual concepts there are, of which we are totally unaware and would never even dream of? This awareness increases our confidence that Hashem's knowledge is infinitely greater, and He certainly knows what He needs to do.

Moshe Rabbeinu asked Hashem the classic question we are currently dealing with: "Why do the righteous sometimes suffer, and the wicked sometimes prosper?" The Gemara's answer is not so clear. That being said, the *Alshich HaKadosh* understands the Gemara to say that a *tzaddik* may be receiving punishment for something he did in a previous *gilgul*. According to this approach, this was Hashem's own explanation to Moshe when asked the question of *tzaddik v'ra lo*!

THE CANTONISTS

Rav Elchonon Wasserman quoted his holy *rebbi*, the Chafetz Chaim: "As is known, the wicked kingdom [of Czar Nikolai, *yemach shemo*] decreed about one hundred and thirty years ago the decree of the Cantonists. They grabbed away by force tender Jewish children and raised them by uncircumsized [non-Jewish] farmers. Afterward, they were forced to serve in the Russian army for no less than twenty-five years. The *Gedolei Yisrael* then were amazed that the meaning of this decree, the likes of which there never had been before, was withheld from them.

However, the Chafetz Chaim, who knew even the concealed secrets of the world, clearly stated the purpose of this decree. In the book of *Shoftim*, in the seventh chapter, we read about the war of Gidon ben Yoash with the Midyanim. There it is told how he chose his men. He led the people down to the water. If someone lapped the water in his hands to drink, he knew he was a *tzaddik*. When someone kneeled on his knees to drink, he knew that he was accustomed to kneeling in front of the *avodah zarah*, and Gidon was instructed not to allow him to fight in the war. From among ten thousand soldiers, only three hundred were found lapping the water and who did not kneel on their knees. Only through them did Hashem give a great salvation to Yisrael. All the rest of them were returned, each man to his place.

Similarly, this shameful occurrence repeated itself during the days of the kingdoms of Yehudah and Yisrael. Even in the days of the First Beis Hamikdash, many Jews were drawn after the *Baalim* and the *Ashtaros*.

The Chafetz Chaim explained: These unfortunate erring souls were brought down again to this world—in the form of the Cantonists—in order to test them a second time. Would they remain faithful to Hashem and His Torah even under harsh conditions? And truthfully, many of them withstood the tests, and in spite of all the suffering and afflictions in the course of the twenty-five years, they remained strong in their Judaism and remained proper Jews."

Rav Elchonon added:

> *From here we see that sometimes one who stumbled in life the first time, they send him down to this world a second time and an additional third time and put him in very difficult tests for his Judaism to withstand...The Gra already hinted to this idea in his hints on the verse, "Behold all these G-d will do twice and three times with a person."*[1]*...It is possible that they will send a neshamah such as this after the passing of thousands of years, similar to the Cantonists from the days of the First Beis Hamikdash...This is a lengthy cheshbon that we cannot grasp...According to this, it is possible that the Yidden in our time period, who need to gird themselves with might and withstand difficult tests to maintain their faithfulness to the Torah, may very well be incarnations of neshamos from many hundreds of years ago, and have come to the world in these times of anger for this very purpose, to withstand the tests and demonstrate clearly that they are firmly rooted Jews.*

---

1   *Iyov* 33:29.

THE SHACH AND THE SPANISH EXPULSION

A similar idea is found in the commentary of the *Shach*[2] on the Torah. The verse says: "The evil will befall you in the end of days."[3] The literal translation of the word "befall" is "it will call you." The *Shach* explains as follows: After the expulsion from Spain in 1492, many of the Jews hoped to find refuge in Portugal. However, it didn't take long before the Portuguese king issued similar decrees as those that had been made in Spain. The king announced that whoever refused to convert would be burned in fire. Some of B'nei Yisrael asked, "Where is the place of fire?" The "evil called them" and they ran. They brought their children and their wives there, rejoicing and with dancing, and threw themselves into the *beis ha'sereifah*. This was because they had desecrated the name of heaven in the days of the *Shoftim*, as it says: "They worshipped the idols, the *Baalim* and the *Ashtaros*." Therefore, they were brought back in a *gilgul* to sanctify the name of heaven in public and were throwing themselves into fire.

The *Shaarei Aharon* comments: "This is astounding! The last of the judges, Eli HaKohen, lived in the third thousand [from Creation], and the incident in Portugal was in the sixth thousand. Almost three thousand years had passed since the time of that sin, and they had still not as yet come to their correction." Chazal have already told us that seven things are concealed from people, and one of them is the depth of the judgment. It says in *Tehillim*: "Your judgments are a great abyss."[4] The *Ibn Ezra* explains that this verse means that "to understand Your judgments is like a great abyss which no one can see the bottom."

We are supposed to try and understand, but our knowledge is, by definition, limited. Without knowing what a soul did in previous incarnations, we really can't judge what it needs to experience now in order to achieve its final *tikkun*.

We have already quoted the *Rambam*, who tells us in *Hilchos Teshuvah* that no one but Hakadosh Baruch Hu, the G-d of infinite intelligence,

---

2 A famous seventeenth-century commentator on *Shulchan Aruch*.
3 *Devarim* 31:29.
4 *Tehillim* 36:7.

can make the judgment of the merits or demerits of any particular individual. He also tells us that sometimes a person is punished in this world, sometimes in the next, and sometimes in both. Hashem knows exactly whom to punish and where. As previously mentioned, even the *malachim* cannot explain the complexity of Hakadosh Baruch Hu's judgments. When we arrive in the world of truth, we will understand better.

Summing Up

We began with a famous—and important—question. Why is it that sometimes we see a *tzaddik* that is afflicted and a wicked person who is successful? We have endeavored to outline some of the principles that could shed light on this. The Torah itself has shared these ideas:

- The purpose of *yissurim* is sometimes to arouse a person to do *teshuvah*.
- Sometimes the purpose of *yissurim* is to purify a person from a sin that he did, in order for him to come "cleansed" to *Olam Haba*, and not need to be purified there.
- There are *yissurim* called *yissurim shel ahavah*, "*yissurim* of love," for no sin at all, just to be a test for a person, to increase his reward in *Olam Haba*. Only the very great *tzaddikim* are given *yissurim shel ahavah*.
- A good person may be removed early from the world in order to prevent him from turning sour, like the story of Chanoch in *Bereishis*.
- A *tzaddik*'s suffering may be for an atonement for his generation, as we saw in the story of the *rebbi* of Reish Lakish's son who was taken as a *korban* for the generation.
- An influential person may be held responsible for not having protested sufficiently against the sinners of his generation.

- Sometimes reward is given to a *rasha* in this world, even for some infinitesimally small good thing that he did.
- A person may be punished for something he did in a previous *gilgul*.
- There are many other such causes, whether known to us through the words of Chazal, or concealed from us and known only to the Creator.

Knowing at least some of the ways by which Hashem conducts the affairs of mankind makes it a little easier to recognize that the Ribbono Shel Olam knows what He is doing.

Of course, to our eyes, there remains a seeming lack of consistency. Think about it:

- Shlomo HaMelech: "There is no righteous man who does only good and never sins."[5] Everyone makes mistakes sometimes. In accordance with the concept that the *tzaddik* is given *yissurim* to be cleansed in this world, we should see every *tzaddik* suffering—but we see no such thing. There are *tzaddikim* who live relatively tranquil lives until their last day!
- We also don't see that every *rasha* prospers, even if he may have done some good things in his life. Some wicked people are actually quite afflicted, lead a fairly tough life, and die young.

So, although we know some general principles, we aren't able to discern any consistent pattern—neither concerning others nor ourselves. We will just have to be satisfied with the general ideas we have gleaned, even though we still walk in relative darkness.

---

5   *Koheles* 7:20.

CHAPTER
SIXTEEN

Can We Judge?

The Chafetz Chaim once said, "If I would have created the world, I would have created it exactly like the Ribbono Shel Olam did because that's the way it is supposed to be!" A petitioner once came to see the Chafetz Chaim, and when the *tzaddik* asked, "How are you?" he responded, "It wouldn't hurt if things were a little bit better." Whereupon the Chafetz Chaim said, "How do you know it wouldn't hurt?" Such is our belief even before we start. We have total confidence that things are the way they are because that's the way they are supposed to be, even when we don't know why.

ALL IN ITS TIME

Shlomo HaMelech tells us that everything has its time: "There is a time for everything and every endeavor under the heavens. A time to bear children and a time to die, etc."[1] This means that everything in life follows the Creator's master plan, which ordains each occurrence in its proper time. Therefore, we are to accept things as they come.

THE MASTER PLAN

Another important point: Do we think that we are actually capable of fathoming the Creator's agenda? Before we can comprehend the details of the world, we would have to understand the master plan in G-d's

---

1   *Koheles* 3:1–2.

agenda. Were we to fully know the master plan, it would be considerably easier to see how the individual components fit in with that plan.

DON'T ASK THE FARMER QUESTIONS

Rav Elchonon Wasserman was martyred *al kiddush Hashem* outside the Kovno ghetto. He was approached by a Jew in the ghetto sometime prior to this. The Yid said to him, "*Nu, rebbi*, what do you say now?" In other words, "Where is G-d now?" Reb Elchonon answered him with a parable:

> Once there were two cousins, one who lived in the city and one who lived on a farm. One time they got together, and the city cousin said to the country cousin, "You know, I've never been to a farm. I'd love to see what you do." The country cousin said, "You can come and watch, but you can't ask any questions because you simply won't understand." The city cousin agreed and came to the farm during plowing season.
>
> The country cousin plowed furrows in a beautiful field of grass, while the city cousin looked on in amazement. "What are you doing? You have a beautiful field, and you're making mud holes!" The farm cousin said, "I told you not to ask. You are not ready to understand."
>
> The country cousin brought out a bag of seed and started throwing the seeds into the furrows. "What are you doing? You're taking perfectly good seed and throwing it into the mud!"
>
> Some time passed; the wheat started to sprout, so the city cousin said, "Oh! Now I see what you did. You produced a beautiful field of wheat!" The farm cousin took a sickle in his hand and started cutting down the wheat. "What are you doing? You finally have something worthwhile, and now you're ruining it!"
>
> The country cousin took the wheat and ground it up. "Why are you making powder out of it? What for?" The farm cousin mixed water into it and turned it into a white mud. The city

cousin asked, "What in the world are you doing? It all doesn't make any sense!"

But when he finally saw the beautiful loaves of bread coming out of the oven, he realized retroactively that there had been a sensible plan here. Each step was part of that master plan to produce bread.

"And so," Reb Elchonon said, "If you don't understand Hakadosh Baruch Hu's master plan, you cannot understand the individual components."

SO TELL US THE MASTER PLAN

The reader might say now, "OK, let's go! Tell us the master plan." Not so fast. It's not all that simple. Although a *maamin* believes that Hakadosh Baruch Hu has a master plan and that everything that happens fits in perfectly to the plan and makes perfect sense, he knows that he can only fathom a tiny bit of Hashem's master plan for the universe. That little bit is what has been revealed to us in the Torah. Everything above and beyond that smattering of information he accepts with perfect confidence, whether he does or does not understand.

HOW SILLY TO JUDGE HASHEM

Modern man, in his extreme arrogance, does not like to admit that there are concepts he cannot understand. He thinks he knows everything. After all, humans have already walked on the moon, discovered DNA, and invented sophisticated computers that can find an answer to almost any question. While modern man doesn't like to admit it, the truth of the matter is that even in science, astronomy, and medicine, we're just scratching the surface. Certainly, in spiritual matters we should not expect that our *seichel* can decide what makes sense and what does not. We are like a little child, a four-year-old boy, who is being brought to the doctor for an inoculation. The boy enters the office happy and smiling. All of a sudden, the doctor pulls out a big needle and is about to inject it in him. The poor child looks askance at his mother, as if to say, "What did I do to deserve this? What's going on?" Can she explain to him that there are diseases called polio, diphtheria, or smallpox, and that this shot will prevent him from getting sick? There is no way for a four-year-old to possibly comprehend such a complex subject. Nor can anyone teach a four-year-old calculus. He just doesn't have the capacity to comprehend.

This is precisely how silly it is for us to think that we can understand and make judgments on Hakadosh Baruch Hu with our puny *seichel*. There are people who think that when they die after 120 years, they're going to go up to the throne of glory to tell Hakadosh Baruch Hu how He should have run the world. They are going to be in for a major surprise when they see that all of their questions will be blown away like so much stubble in the wind. It never happened that someone debated with Hakadosh Baruch Hu and won. If we could ask Hakadosh Baruch Hu the questions we're asking here and get His response, you can be sure that the questions would simply disappear. He would show us how much we didn't begin to understand of what this world is really all about. He would surely say to us, "What do you understand, what do you know? Do you know the essence of the *neshamah*, the reality of the World to Come, the meaning of eternity? You simply don't understand the entire matter from top to bottom."

HASHEM IS ALWAYS RIGHT

We never sit in judgment on Hakadosh Baruch Hu because it simply makes no sense to do so. A young child may not understand why his parents insist that he goes to school and why they bother him to learn letters that he sees no purpose in. Even if his parents will attempt to explain to him that someday he's going to get bigger and will need to be able to read, the child may still think that he could do very well just staying home and playing with his blocks. He just doesn't have the maturity to understand. Relatively speaking, we have much less intelligence than that child to understand Hakadosh Baruch Hu's ways and His system.

The purpose of what we write here is not to justify what happens in the world and certainly not to decide whether we think Hakadosh Baruch Hu is fair or not. When Yirmiyahu HaNavi was seemingly debating with Hashem concerning the tremendous success that Hashem had granted the wicked Nevuchadnetzar, he said, "You are right, Hashem, when I argue with You. But [nevertheless] I will speak judgments with You. Why is the way of the wicked so successful, all the evildoers are tranquil?"[2]

In other words, when I ask a *kashya*, I know You are right even before I start. But I just want to understand. We, too, start with the premise that Hakadosh Baruch Hu is right, fair, and just. Our inability to comprehend the happenings of this world with our puny *seichel* does not detract one iota from His correctness. Hakadosh Baruch Hu knows infinitely better than we do how the world needs to be run. Our hope is merely to understand as much as we are able to.

THERE REALLY ARE NO QUESTIONS

There is a story told about the *Ramban*. He had made an agreement with a *chaver* that whichever of the two would die first would come back to the other in a dream and let him know what happened in his judgment. I don't think that simple people can make such deals, but obviously the *Ramban* could. So, sure enough, when the friend was about to die, the *Ramban* went to him and said, "Don't forget our agreement. Come back and report to me how your judgment went. However, once you're coming back anyway, please bring me an answer to an *emunah* question that puzzles me," after which he explained the question.

Sure enough, the friend was *niftar*, and after *shivah* he came to the *Ramban* in a dream to report how his judgment had gone. "But," he said, "as far as your question is concerned, I have no answer. When I got to the world of truth, everything was so crystal clear, I couldn't remember what the difficulty was."

All our questions are only in this world, which is one of confusing darkness. In the world of truth, there are no questions because everything will be absolutely clear.

---

2   *Yirmiyahu* 12:1.

Summing Up

To sum up what we've said so far: While the meager information offered here gives us only a partial answer to our question, nevertheless, we can be confident and at peace because we rely on the infinite intelligence of the Creator that there is a master plan. He knows what He is doing, and there are very deep calculations here that are concealed from us because our mortal minds are simply too limited and small to grasp them.

Soon, we will try to clarify additional issues that puzzle us about Divine providence.

CHAPTER
SEVENTEEN

Teshuvah

Although this book is not specifically about *teshuvah*, we would surely be remiss if we did not shed a little light on the atonement that can be achieved through *teshuvah*, thus circumventing the need for *yissurim*. Even if a person has not lived up to his potential and has committed *aveiros*, all hope is not lost. There is always *teshuvah*.

The ability to erase our sins with *teshuvah* is something that human logic cannot easily grasp. Once the improper deed has been committed and the harm has been done, how is it possible to remove it retroactively? That, however, is the great *chessed* of *teshuvah*, that indeed the *aveiros* are erased.

When a person leaves this world, he is shown a review of everything he did in this life, somewhat like a video: "When a person leaves this world, all his deeds are enumerated before him, and it is said to him, 'Such and such you did in such and such a place on such and such a day.'"[1] How fortunate is the person who did only things he can be proud of, and how unfortunate is the person who performed deeds of which he will then be ashamed. The awesome kindness of *teshuvah* is that the video can be edited. Any sins for which we did proper *teshuvah* are erased from the record as if they never took place. They will never be mentioned during our judgment, and we will not be punished for them.

---

1   *Taanis* 11a.

After the destruction of the First Beis Hamikdash, the Jews came to Yechezkel HaNavi and said that they would like to make amends but that they didn't believe that *teshuvah* could help. He reassured them in the name of Hashem that *teshuvah* would indeed erase all their sins. Such is the great *chessed* of *teshuvah*. "When the *rasha* repents from his sins that he did and keeps My laws…all his sins that he did shall not be mentioned to him."[2]

The great Tanna Rabbi Eliezer tells us, "Do *teshuvah* one day before you die."[3] His *talmidim* asked him, "Does a person know on which day he will die?"[4] He answered, "All the more reason that he should do *teshuvah* today because perhaps he will die tomorrow." If Rabbi Eliezer wanted to tell us to do *teshuvah* every day because it might be our last day, why didn't he just say, "Do *teshuvah* every day?"

Rabbi Eliezer is teaching us a great lesson here, of great relevance to our subject. Without question, we should do *teshuvah* every day so that no sins will remain on our record. However, the most important time for *teshuvah* is before death so that when we go for our final judgment, our record will be clear. Therefore, we must do *teshuvah* every day since we don't know which day will be our last.

Rabbi Eliezer continues: "Shlomo said in his wisdom, 'At all times your garments shall be clean, nor should there lack oil on your head.'"[5] He compares this to a king who invited his servants to a feast but did not specify the time. The fools confidently went out to their work in the fields, assuming that it would take a long time to prepare such a feast. The wise ones went to get dressed and ready, knowing that the large staff in the royal kitchen could whip up a feast in a short time. When the announcement came to attend the feast, the fools had no choice but to come improperly groomed, thereby enraging the king. We, too, must realize that someday we may be called suddenly, and we must

---

2   *Yechezkel* 18:21–22.
3   *Avos* 2:15.
4   *Shabbos* 153a.
5   *Koheles* 9:8.

make sure that we have cleansed ourselves from our sins before that moment comes.

This concept of *teshuvah* is very relevant to what we have written here. As we have already said, there are few people who never make mistakes, but when they do, there is a way to erase them.

RAMBAM

The *Rambam* also emphasizes the importance of repenting before death: "Since every person has free will, as we have clarified, a person should endeavor to do *teshuvah* and confess with his mouth all his sins and shake his hands clean of his sins in order to die a *baal teshuvah* and merit the afterlife."[6]

> ## Summing Up
> The ability to cleanse our sins through *teshuvah* is an awesome kindness from our Creator. It can alleviate the necessity for *yissurim*.

---

6   *Teshuvah* 7:1.

CHAPTER
EIGHTEEN

Community versus Individual

Now that we have gained some degree of insight into the factors that can cause an individual to undergo travails, our next task is to discuss the ways in which Hakadosh Baruch Hu deals with a community. This may refer to a small town, a larger city, an entire nation, or even the whole world. What happens to the individual when there is a decree of retribution on a community?

Certainly, in every community there are those who are on a more elevated level than that of the individuals who brought about the harsh decree. If everyone in that place would be like those better ones, the evil decree would not have come. Why doesn't Hashem "punish" only those who need "correction" and leave the *tzaddikim* alone?

One of the reasons must certainly be that doing so would negate free will. If Hashem were to save all the better ones and only destroy the ones whose sins brought about the decree, the Divine providence would be too obvious. Therefore, there is now a new decision made in heaven on the better people. True, it wasn't their sins that brought about the *tzaros*. However, are they deserving of the special treatment of being singled out to be saved? Hashem will make this judgment on each individual and decide who will survive the calamity and who will not.

Based on many factors, not every person who is not at fault for bringing the calamity is deserving of being saved. Therefore, when there is a judgment on a *tzibbur*, each person is judged not only according to his personal status but also according to his status within the greater community. Any *tzaddik* who perished because he was part of a sinful community will be amply recompensed in *Olam Haba*.

This concept appears early in world history.

- Prior to the great *mabul*, Hashem said to Noach, "The end of *all* flesh has come before me."[1] *Rashi* explains: "Wherever you find the sins of immorality and *avodah zarah*, a wave of punishment comes to the world and kills the *good* and the *bad*." The "good" here doesn't mean the truly righteous. It means the ones who also sinned, but not as severely as the others. The catastrophe didn't come because of them, but still they were not worthy of being singled out to be saved.

- In Mitzrayim, the Jews were told to stay indoors all night because "Once permission is given to the destroyer to destroy, he doesn't differentiate between the righteous and the wicked."[2] When the teacher punishes his class because they didn't behave, then the ones who weren't so out of order will also have to suffer. This is the way the Ribbono Shel Olam runs His world.

- When Avraham Avinu was informed that Hashem was about to destroy the city of Sodom, he begged and pleaded with Hakadosh Baruch Hu to save them. The city of Sodom was the epitome of wickedness, immorality, *avodah zarah*, and cruelty. Nevertheless, Avraham Avinu prayed that they should be spared. Avraham said, "Hashem! Will You in Your anger also destroy the righteous with the wicked? Maybe there are fifty *tzaddikim* in the city. Will you destroy in Your anger and not bear this place for the sake of the fifty *tzaddikim* in it?"[3] In other words, Hashem should forgive the whole city in the merit of the *tzaddikim*! "It is profane

---

1 *Bereishis* 6:13.
2 *Bava Kama* 60a.
3 *Bereishis* 18:23–25.

to You to do such a thing, to kill the *tzaddik* with the *rasha*. Will the Judge of the whole earth not do justice?" *Rashi* explains that Avraham first asked to spare the whole city in the merit of the fifty *tzaddikim*. Then he asked that, at least, Hashem should not kill the *tzaddikim* with the *resha'im*. This, to Avraham Avinu's mind, is seemingly inappropriate. After all, He is the Judge of the whole world. Such an unfair thing cannot be! It is a contradiction in terms. Hashem said, "If I find in Sodom fifty *tzaddikim* in the city, I will bear the entire place because of them." Avraham continued to ask for even less than fifty. What if there are forty-five? Hashem agrees to forty-five, then forty, thirty, twenty, and ten. Avraham didn't ask for less than ten. That was the end of the discussion, and the *malach* was sent to destroy Sodom.

There are considerable difficulties with this last point:

- Does Avraham think he will teach Hashem what's fair and what's not? Avraham understands better than anyone that Hakadosh Baruch Hu knows what He needs to do, even when we don't comprehend it. If Hakadosh Baruch Hu told him that He must destroy the city, then that is the way it has to be. Is Avraham going to argue with Hashem and lecture Him about fairness?
- To Avraham's mind it is an unresolvable contradiction that the Judge of the whole earth should kill the *tzaddikim*! It's just unthinkable, impossible! How could it be that Avraham did not realize what was most obvious—that there simply were no *tzaddikim* in the city, and that was why Hashem was prepared to destroy the whole city? Someone standing near Avraham at that moment would have whispered in his ear, "Reb Avraham, Hashem told you He's going to destroy these cities. You don't know if there are any *tzaddikim* in the city. To your mind, if there would be *tzaddikim*, Hashem would have to save them, and maybe even save the entire city for their sake. So, if Hashem told you that He is destroying the city, isn't it obvious that there are no *tzaddikim* there?" When Avraham davened, he only said "maybe" there are *tzaddikim* there. He didn't know if there actually were

any *tzaddikim*. The truth was that there really weren't any. The people of Sodom were all wicked. So how could he question what Hashem was doing because of a "maybe?"
- When Hashem responded favorably to his *tefillah*, saying, "OK, I'll save the city if I find the *tzaddikim* because I am accepting your prayer," was Avraham then happy? No! This implied that if Avraham hadn't prayed, Hashem wouldn't have spared the *tzaddikim*, and Avraham's philosophical issue remained unresolved. How could Hashem have even considered destroying the *tzaddikim* with the *resha'im*? Can the "Judge of the whole world not do justice?"

This is a very difficult exchange for us to understand.

DRAWING A CONCLUSION

It seems quite clear that Avraham Avinu did *not* know if there were any righteous people in Sodom. But what he did know was that even if there were *tzaddikim* in the city, they might have perished along with the wicked of the city because that is how Hakadosh Baruch Hu runs the world. He straightens out all the accounts in *Olam Haba*, and no one gets cheated.

If this is the case, and of course knowing that Avraham knew of Hashem's righteousness and perfection much more than we do, why did Avraham plead and argue with Hakadosh Baruch Hu? Why not just trust that Hashem knows best?

The answer seems to be that Heavenly judgments are made as if on a big scale:

- On one side of the scale, there are the negative points.
- On the other side of the scale, there are the positive points.

There are countless points on both sides. Theoretically, Hakadosh Baruch Hu also agrees that Heavenly justice should decree that the righteous always be spared. Each one should be judged exclusively by his own personal record, without taking into account that he finds himself in a city upon which there is a decree of destruction. However, Hashem's wisdom declares that this cannot always be the case because it would negate free will, or for various other reasons. In each situation, a decision must be made about whether to take into account that "the Judge of the whole world must do justice" versus the necessity to use that factor sparingly so as not to interfere with free will. Therefore, Hashem puts both factors on their respective sides of the scale. Sometimes He will indeed save the more righteous one, and sometimes not. Sometimes the *tzaddik* deserves special treatment, and sometimes the *tzaddik* will not get the special treatment of being saved. Indeed, one of the calculations on that big scale is, "Will the Judge of the whole world not do justice?" However, that's only one factor, but there are many other factors on the opposite side of the scale.

When the *tzaddik* (in this case, Avraham) davens, his prayer is added to the consideration of treating the *tzaddik* with justice, according to his own merits. His *tefillah* adds weight to that factor. Sometimes, the *tefillah* on behalf of a *tzaddik* will add sufficient weight to tip the scale to the side of merit. When Avraham said it would not be fair to destroy the righteous with the wicked, he was not intending to "teach" Hakadosh Baruch Hu about fairness. He was merely echoing one of the factors that Hakadosh Baruch Hu Himself takes into account and puts on the Heavenly scale.

Summing Up

The Heavenly scale is much too complex for us humans to understand. Nevertheless, we have been taught that individuals are judged not only on their own merits and demerits, but also as part of a community. *B'ezras Hashem*, as we continue, we will see that this concept will make a big difference in understanding the entire history of the Jewish People.

CHAPTER
NINETEEN

Historical Churban

If the issue of an individual *tzaddik*'s suffering causes people to have doubts, and the sufferings of particular communities add extra questions (addressed above), how much more so will the collective sufferings of the Jewish People as a nation weaken people's confidence in the ways of Hashem. No nation has ever been so repeatedly persecuted, banished, discriminated against, and demonized as our people have been. Not only in the past, but in the present as well. In stark contrast to the truth, we are accused of racism, apartheid, and oppression against terrorists whose sole aim in life is to destroy us. Is it any wonder that some people become disillusioned and begin to think that there is no fairness in the world? No thinking individual can ignore the question of why Hashem decreed such a destiny for His chosen people. How helpful and comforting it would be to have even some perspective on this. Later in this book, we will devote a chapter to the issue of why the Jewish People have been singled out for hardships. Now we will discuss the pattern of individual tragedies that have befallen us.

Thankfully, we have sources that help us understand this phenomenon, at least somewhat. Concerning tragedies that occurred in the era of the *Tanach*, we have insights directly from the *nevi'im*. Chazal clarified for us precisely what happened and why. Remember that when we look at incidents in *Tanach*, we are seeing world happenings not from a human perspective but from the perspective of the Creator. Some things may always remain a mystery, but at least we will get to see how Hashem responds in certain types of situations.

Of course, in fairness, we must acknowledge from the outset how easy it is to sit in comfort and speak about this. The agony, fright, pain, and horror that our people have gone through cannot be understated. The multitudes who perished, and the shattered lives of those who survived, defy expression in words. Whoever endured these historical horrors surely endured what can be called Gehinnom on earth. Nothing that we say here is meant to diminish our sorrow for them and what they suffered.

Nevertheless, we are meant to try to understand the *darchei Hashem* and what the Torah tells us about such occurrences as well as possible, no matter how painful it is to delve into the subject.

In order to begin comprehending, we must first study the pattern of *how* Hashem works when He brings hard times upon us. Then we can ask the subsequent *why* questions and see whatever we can come up with. The following pattern seems to emanate from a review of the national tragedies that have come upon Klal Yisrael:

- Hashem judges the community by the majority. If they are found lacking, a harsh decree may come upon the community as a whole.[1]
- When a community is punished, the more righteous among them may perish as well. This may include even young children and babies.
- Some members of the community may survive, but we will not necessarily be able to discern any pattern of who does or does not survive. Indeed, there was never a calamity in which there was a noticeable pattern of differentiation between the *tzaddikim* and the non-*tzaddikim*.

---

1   Rambam, Teshuvah 3:2.

- Anyone who is personally righteous but suffers because they were found among a sinful community will be amply reimbursed in *Olam Haba*.
- Traditionally, Jews never asked, "Where was G-d?" in their travails. Rather they sought out their own faults, said *viduy*, and confessed their sins.
- Even a great sinner that is killed because he is a Jew receives atonement for all his sins and has a share in the afterlife.[2]

NOTHING "JUST HAPPENS"

We can never ask, "Where was Hashem?" in times of calamity. Nothing happens in the world without His knowledge and control, and He never goes on vacation. This is one of the basic building blocks of belief in Hashem, and we cannot attribute any historical occurrence to chance or to any other cause but the Creator. Everything is done with Hakadosh Baruch Hu's exacting *Hashgachah*. He is always there, whether we understand what is happening or we don't, whether we like what is happening or we don't.

This thought is clearly expressed by *Rambam*.[3]

> *It is a positive command from the Torah to cry out and to blow the trumpets [in the Beis Hamikdash] whenever a trouble comes on the tzibbur. As is stated: "You should blow the trumpets over anything which will distress you,"[4] such as a drought or a pestilence or a plague of locusts or such things. Cry out and blow the trumpets. This thing is one of the ways of teshuvah, for in a time when a tzarah comes and they cry out on it and they blow the trumpets, everyone will know that it is because of their evil deeds that bad things have happened to them. As it says: "It is your sins that have brought all of these about."[5] That is what will cause them to remove the tzarah from upon*

---

2   *Sanhedrin* 47b.
3   *Hilchos Taanis* 1:1–3.
4   *Bamidbar* 10:9.
5   *Yirmiyahu* 5:25.

themselves. But if they don't cry out and they don't blow the Chatzotzros, and instead they say [that] this is merely the custom of the world that has happened to us, this tzarah is just an occurrence, and it's a coincidence, this is a way of cruelty because it will cause them to cling to their evil deeds even more, and this tzarah will bring other tzaros with it. This is what is written in the Torah, that when I bring a tzarah on you that you should do teshuvah, "If you go with me with keri, which means you say, 'It's just an accidental happening,' then I will go with you with the anger that you caused by saying it's just a happening, and you will have more tzaros."[6]

Let us review some of the tragic *churbanos* of old and see if we can discern the abovementioned pattern.

THE GOLDEN CALF

We wrote earlier that Hashem deals with us not only on an individual level but on a communal level as well. When a segment of the people made a golden calf forty days after *Matan Torah*, the entire Jewish People was held liable for it. Hashem said, "Leave Me alone, and My anger will be kindled on them, and I will destroy them and make you into a great nation."[7] He hinted that Moshe could daven for them and thus save them.[8] Hence, if not for Moshe's pleading for them, the entire people would have been included in this decree of total annihilation, even many of our greatest and most righteous, such as Yehoshua, Aharon, Miriam, Nachshon ben Aminadav, the tribe of Levi, the women, the children, and the babies. Everybody! Hakadosh Baruch Hu's anger was against the *tzibbur* as a whole. Not one member of the tribe of Levi had been guilty of the sin of the golden calf, the women had refused to give their earrings for it, and certainly, the babies had no part in it. Nevertheless, the whole Jewish People would have been destroyed. These are explicit

---

6   *Vayikra* 26:27–28.
7   *Shemos* 32:10.
8   Rashi, *Shemos* 32:10.

verses in the Torah with no room for misinterpretation: the entire Klal Yisrael would have been destroyed had Moshe Rabbeinu not intervened.

For us, this has a familiar ring. It strongly resembles what we said concerning Avraham Avinu when he davened for Sodom. Although he wasn't sure if there were any *tzaddikim* in Sodom, he knew that if Hakadosh Baruch Hu's intention was to destroy the city, that might include even the *tzaddikim*. If the *tzibbur* as a whole was found guilty, not every *tzaddik* would be saved—perhaps even none. Hashem's calculations are beyond our capacity to understand, but as we review the historical travails of our people, we will discover that this is the basic pattern in all that has befallen our people throughout the ages.

Although only a small minority actually worshipped the golden calf, perhaps the rest of the nation was considered guilty for not protesting and stopping them. After all, they were the vast majority. They should have risen up in unison and said, "No, we don't let you! You cannot make any idols here!" Then, the *aveirah* and consequent destruction would never have happened. For their failure to do so, the people were held as guilty as if they had worshipped the idol themselves. Therefore, the decree was on the Jewish People as a whole. (This is no surprise because we have already shown that one who can prevent a sin through rebuking, but neglects doing so, is considered as if he had committed the sin himself.)

The golden calf was not an *avodah zarah* in the sense of a pagan god, as one might mistakenly glean from a superficial reading. Its worshippers surely did not think that the calf itself had taken them out of Egypt! The verse makes it clear that it was not an exchange for Hashem at all, but merely a replacement for Moshe Rabbeinu. The Divine presence had been with Moshe Rabbeinu, but now even he seemed to have disappeared, so Klal Yisrael sought an image upon which they hoped the Divine presence would rest. When Aharon made the golden calf, he tried to stall for time in the hope that Moshe would come back before they worshipped it. In order to delay them, he said, "Tomorrow will be a festival for Hashem."[9] Seemingly he should have said, "Tomorrow will be a festival for the calf," but he did not because the golden calf was merely considered a go-between for the people to connect to Hashem. There are many explanations there as to why the people then thought that the Shechinah would rest on this idol. None of these justified what they did, however, because it is absolutely clear that the prohibition of idolatry includes using the idol as an intermediary. Those who worshipped Hashem via the golden calf transgressed the prohibition of idolatry, to the same degree as if they had believed that the idol was the god that created the universe.

THE SIN OF THE SPIES

Hashem had intended that Klal Yisrael would enter Eretz Yisrael immediately. The spies whom the people sent came back and discouraged them from going. They frightened the nation by describing the heavily fortified cities in Canaan and the presence of giants among them. The spies insisted that it was simply impossible to conquer the Land.

The people became frightened and disillusioned, complaining that they never should have been taken out of Egypt in the first place. Hakadosh Baruch Hu was angry with them because His miracles had accompanied them from the moment Moshe Rabbeinu came to Mitzrayim. They should have known that Hashem loved them and that they could put their trust in Him. But instead of silencing the spies, they cried. Once again, Hashem threatened to destroy the entire nation. When Moshe davened for them, Hashem lightened the decree:

- They would not die immediately, but rather they would have to wander in the desert for forty years.
- The men who were over twenty at the time would all die in the desert when they reached age sixty.
- Those younger than twenty at that time would not have to die in the desert.
- The women were not held responsible; they would enter Eretz Yisrael.

---

9   *Shemos* 32:5.

- The tribe of Levi was not held guilty for the sin of the *meraglim* since they had not sent a spy.

There are two very important lessons here. Had Moshe Rabbeinu not davened for them, the entire Klal Yisrael would have been destroyed, just as we saw in the case of the golden calf. Even after Moshe's *tefillah*, those who were not held responsible (and were not destined to die in the desert) still had to wait out the forty years to get into Eretz Yisrael. Hashem did not say that those who hadn't participated in the sin of the *meraglim* could enter Eretz Yisrael right away, as was the original plan. The youth, the women, and the tribe of Levi would all have to bear the decree. Even Kalev and Yehoshua had to wait out the forty years. Klal Yisrael would enter Eretz Yisrael as a whole, as a nation. If the nation was not worthy, the minority of the nation would not go into Eretz Yisrael.

This can be likened to the *rebbi* who punishes his class for misbehavior and tells them they have forfeited the trip he promised them. One boy who had been very well-behaved says, "*Rebbi*, I didn't misbehave." The *rebbi* replies, "I'll reward you in some other way, but I'm not taking you on the trip. The trip is for the class, and the class doesn't deserve it."

ZECHARIAH HANAVI

About two hundred years before the *churban* of the First Beis Hamikdash, there was a king, Yehoash, from the dynasty of David HaMelech, whose life was in danger. He was saved and protected by the Kohen Gadol Yehoyada. He was hidden in the attic above the *Kodesh HaKodashim* for six years. Astoundingly, when Yehoyada died, the leaders of Yehudah began to worship Yehoash as divine—after all, he had been hidden above the *Kodesh HaKodashim* for six years and had not been harmed!

Yehoyada's son, Zechariah, rose up in the courtyard of the Beis Hamikdash on Yom Kippur to rebuke the people. Yehoash had his men murder him in cold blood right there in the *Azarah*. As Zechariah was dying, he said, "Hashem will see and seek [revenge for my blood]."[10]

---

10 *Divrei Hayamim II* 24:22.

For the next two hundred years, nothing they did could wash away Zechariah's blood, which bubbled incessantly. The Gemara records that when Nevuchadnetzar's chief executioner, Nevuzaradan, entered the Beis Hamikdash, he inquired about the blood.[11] When they finally admitted what had happened, Nevuzaradan said he would appease Zechariah. He slaughtered the elders of the highest Sanhedrin and other Sanhedrins, young and old men, women and *cheder* children. He murdered one million, one hundred thousand Jews in a certain valley, and nine hundred thousand more in Yerushalayim. The blood still did not stop bubbling. Finally, he said, "Zechariah! Zechariah! I killed the best of them. Do you want me to kill them all?" When he said this, the blood stopped bubbling.

Yirmiyahu HaNavi wrote: "Remember, Hashem, and look down [to see] to whom you have done so. If women can eat their own offspring..."[12] The verse ends: "If a priest and a prophet can be killed in the Mikdash of Hashem." Hashem responded to his complaint: "Was it right for you to kill Zechariah, a priest and a prophet, right in the courtyard of the Beis Hamikdash?"

That Zechariah's blood was bubbling was a public demonstration of the Heavenly accusation against the Jewish People. That alone should have sufficed to bring about a wave of *teshuvah*. The *teshuvah* wasn't forthcoming, and Zechariah's blood demanded retribution. The Creator does not tolerate such atrocities among His chosen people.

THE TEN TRIBES

The *Tanach* records that as a punishment for certain sins, Shlomo HaMelech was informed that after his death the Jewish People would be divided into two nations:

- Yehudah and Binyamin would be to the south, in the kingdom of Yehudah.
- The ten remaining tribes would be to the north, in the kingdom of Yisrael.

---

11 *Gittin* 57b.
12 *Eichah* 2:20.

The ten tribes turned wayward immediately. Their first king set up two golden calves as an alternative to the Beis Hamikdash, one in the north of his kingdom and one in the south, near the border to Eretz Yehudah. He put police at the border to prevent his people from going back to the Beis Hamikdash for Yom Tov. Anyone trying to cross the border was to be killed, in an effort to coerce the people into worshipping his golden calves. In the course of two hundred and fifty years plus that this kingdom was in existence, not one of the kings abandoned the practice of worshipping at these two idolatrous shrines. As time went on, they strayed even more into other sins.

There were many *nevi'im* living among the ten tribes, including some of the *nevi'im* whose prophecies are recorded in the book of *Trei Asar*. They warned the people repeatedly in the name of Hashem, telling them over and over again that they would be severely punished; the enemy would come, wreak destruction on the land, and murder many people. Then they would be forced out of Eretz Yisrael. All this came true when, finally, the ten tribes were exiled by the king of Ashur (about one hundred and thirty years before the destruction of the first Beis Hamikdash). To this day we do not know exactly where they are.

The book of *Melachim* includes a very long chapter about how severely they had sinned—especially with *avodah zarah*—and about how Hashem sent the *nevi'im* repeatedly to chastise them. They had no right to complain about what befell them because they were warned again and again. It was as if Hakadosh Baruch Hu was saying, "I waited and I sent my *nevi'im* and the people didn't listen. Now I'm driving them out."

Sancheriv, king of Ashur, was the archenemy of our people at that time. Five-sixths of our people made up the ten tribes, whom he either killed or exiled. Yet Yeshayah HaNavi wrote a striking verse about Sancheriv that gives us an insight on how to look at such happenings: "Woe! Ashur: the staff of My wrath and the stick of My anger on them."[13] Sancheriv was extremely arrogant and he attributed all his victories to his own brilliance. In response to his vanity, Hashem says: "Can the

---

13 *Yeshayah* 10:5.

ax be arrogant over the one who chops with it? Can the saw consider himself greater than the one who moves it?"[14]

Hakadosh Baruch Hu was saying to Sancheriv, "You are nothing but a tool in My hands. I brought this all about. I gave you the power to conquer." Sancheriv was a *rasha* and a bitter enemy of our people. We have every right to hate him, but that doesn't detract one iota from the fact that he was merely a tool in the hands of Hakadosh Baruch Hu.

FAIRLY DECENT PEOPLE

What were the people of the ten tribes like, that they were so severely punished? Were they, perhaps, cannibals or mafia men?

The people of the ten tribes were nothing of the sort. Certainly, they had faults—mostly in the realm of *avodah zarah*, which was the great temptation of the time. Understandably, when there is *avodah zarah*, there are other *aveiros* as well. Even one of their worst kings, Achav, had many good qualities. While he worshipped the Baal and did some other bad things, he had a reputation for benevolence. When there was a war with Aram, Ben Hadad, the king of Aram, was cornered. His men advised him to surrender, saying, "We have heard that the kings of Yisrael are kings of kindness."[15] They put up the white flag and surrendered. Achav said, "Ben Hadad is my brother,"[16] and he sent him home. Predictably, Ben Hadad didn't show any gratitude for the favor and soon came back to attack. But the kings of Yisrael were kings whose reputation of *chessed* spread even to the surrounding nations, and their people revered them. When Achav died, there was a massive funeral for him because the people genuinely mourned him.

Indeed, the people of the ten tribes had many good qualities. There is a story told about them shortly before they were sent into exile.[17] The two countries, Yehudah and Yisrael, competed for sovereignty all the years, with times of peace and times of war. At this particular time, the two countries were at war. The king of Yehudah at that time, Achaz, was

---

14 *Yeshayah* 10:15.
15 *Melachim I* 20:21.
16 *Melachim I* 20:32.
17 *Divrei Hayamim II* 28:8–15.

a terrible *rasha*, and as punishment from Hashem, Yehudah suffered a horrendous massacre on the battlefield: one hundred and twenty thousand of Yehudah's soldiers were slain in just one day. The victorious army of Yisrael took two hundred thousand women and children captive from Yehudah for slaves. They were bringing the captives back to their capital, Shomron, when Oded HaNavi came out to greet the returning army. He said to them, "Yehudah lost because of their sins. With the anger of Hashem on Yehudah, He gave them into your hands. You murdered them with tremendous anger which reached toward the heavens. Do you think now that you're going to take the B'nei Yehudah for slaves and maidservants? You have your own bundles of sins to Hashem your G-d! So listen to me now and return the captives that you've captured from your brethren because Hashem is very angry at you." The leaders of these tribes arose and said, "Do not bring the slaves here because we have enough sins of our own. We don't need to add this to our bundle of sins." They took the people they had captured, dressed them, fed them, and gave them to drink. Those who needed transportation were given donkeys and brought back across the border to their brothers in Yericho.

This gives us an idea of the ten tribes shortly before they were exiled. The return of two hundred thousand slaves would make headlines in any newspaper. These are the people that Hakadosh Baruch Hu was, so to speak, fed up with. Mafia men? Cannibals? Criminals? Absolutely not! Of course, they did have many faults in addition to idolatry, including tendencies toward drunkenness and indulgence. But had we known them, we might have considered them basically nice people! When Sancheriv came shortly after this story, they went through great suffering. Many were killed, and the rest were dispersed in exile. The *nevi'im* said repeatedly that this was all coming to them for their sins.

The point is that when we study *Tanach*, we are seeing cause and effect in the world through Hakadosh Baruch Hu's eyes. Not through our eyes, because our vision is clouded by other factors that we think are playing a role, be they financial, political, or military factors. Hakadosh Baruch Hu is telling us that He was manipulating all of those factors behind the scenes to bring about His agenda—what He has to do with us based on what we have done with Him.

THE FIRST STAGE OF GALUS BAVEL

The first stage of exile from Eretz Yehudah took place a mere eleven years before the destruction of the First Beis Hamikdash. At that time, King Yechanya was taken away, along with a thousand of the top *talmidei chachamim* of Yerushalayim.[18] Although there were many idol worshippers and sinners among the people of Yehudah, there were still numerous *tzaddikim* as well. Among those scholars were some of our greatest men of antiquity, including Mordechai and Yechezkel HaNavi. These *chachamim* are called *"hecharash v'hamasger,"* which means, as the Gemara explains, that they left people "speechless" and "locked up": their wisdom was so great that when they spoke, everyone would become speechless, and when they closed a subject, it was locked permanently because there was nothing to add. Mordechai and Yechezkel were youngsters when they went into exile, and these *chachamim* were their peer group. Not many cities today could produce a thousand such superlative *talmidei chachamim*, not even the greatest Torah centers. This was the Yerushalayim of old, which the *nevi'im* blasted as sinful because, despite the quantity of great people among them, Hashem expected more from them.

The Gemara tells us that exiling this group in advance was actually a great kindness that Hashem did for the Jewish People.[19] Eleven years later, when the bulk of the nation was exiled, they found an entire infrastructure of shuls and yeshivos waiting for them in Bavel. As a result, Bavel remained one of the main centers of Torah for well over a thousand years.

There is an important lesson to be learned here. It was certainly not a pleasant experience for people such as Mordechai and Yechezkel to be led off by Nevuchadnetzar's armies into forced exile. While ultimately this was a great favor for the Jewish nation as a whole, it was very difficult for the exiles to be uprooted from their homes and undergo

---

18 *Melachim II* 24:14.
19 *Gittin* 88a.

all the discomforts of *galus*. This is another dimension of the pattern through which Hashem brings suffering upon his people. Sometimes even our greatest people are called on to make sacrifices for the benefit of their people, bear difficulties, and eventually be amply rewarded for their sufferings.

THE TOCHACHAH

The sections we call *Tochachah* ("chastisement") appear twice in the Torah.[20] In those portions, Hakadosh Baruch Hu warns us and foretells precisely what will befall us if we do not listen to Him and keep the covenant we accepted: the contract we "signed" when we stood at Har Sinai.

What we derive from both of these *parshiyos* is the following message: if we listen to the *d'var Hashem* and fulfill the Torah that we agreed to keep, everything will be very good for the Jewish People. We will be on top of the world and admired by all, with all the accompanying material blessings. However, if we sin and depart from the way of Hashem, it will be very bitter for us. The Torah paints a frightening picture of terrible retribution for us. Every line predicts calamities. We read about sicknesses, defeat in war, and failing crops, resulting in hunger. Wild animals will attack us, and the sword will come upon us from the enemy. Our cities will be besieged, and in the siege we will experience plague and hunger. In starvation, people will even eat their own children, *Rachmana litzlan*. The cities will be deserted and destroyed, we will be scattered into *galus* among the nations, and the sword will chase us even after we go into exile. Our enemies will continue to pursue us relentlessly, and we will live in a state of fear in the land of our enemies. Each of the aforementioned possibilities is a nightmare in and of itself.

In the book of *Devarim*, additional punishments are predicted: "Your carcasses will be for the animals and the birds to eat, and no one will be there to chase away the animals." Numerous verses describe slavery under the yoke of the enemy even while still in our land. We will be pillaged and robbed and unable to resist. Sons and daughters will be given away to other people, taken into captivity. "You will go crazy from

---

20   *Vayikra* 26:14–45, *Devarim* 28:15–69.

what your eyes see." All your fortified cities will be put under siege. Each and every detail is frightening and horrible.[21] The *Ramban* explains that these two portions describe the respective destructions of the first and second commonwealths and Batei Mikdash:

- The first *churban* fulfilled all the details related in *Vayikra*.
- The second *churban* fulfilled all the details related in *Devarim*.

Ramban demonstrates this by going through the two portions detail by detail and showing how the two portions portray precisely what happened at these two times in our history and how the Torah forewarned us as to what will happen if we stray. We know when these calamaties took place, which sins they came for, and on whom those warnings were indeed fulfilled. Obviously, if we have access to this information, the sensible thing for us to do is to analyze carefully the message of the *Tochachah* and what subsequently transpired. Then we will have somewhat of an idea of what Hakadosh Baruch Hu expects of us and what type of actions can elicit such a severe Heavenly response. This will also give us a glimpse of how Hashem reacts to us when we have fallen below His minimum level of expectation. Without this, it is impossible to even hope to begin understanding these matters.

THE FIRST BEIS HAMIKDASH

Chazal tell us that the First Beis Hamikdash was destroyed for idolatry, immorality, and shedding of blood, based on various verses in *Tanach*. At the time of the First Beis Hamikdash, the sin requiring the most frequent rebuke by the *nevi'im* was that of idol worship. Although to us the entire concept of bowing to a manmade idol seems as silly as can be, that was the prevailing *yetzer hara* of the time. It was an almost irresistible temptation, attracting not only simple people but even very wise people. They managed, somehow, to rationalize the blatant contradiction between keeping mitzvos and worshipping *avodah zarah*. Although one who worships *avodah zarah* is considered as one who transgressed the entire Torah, they believed that one could only get

---

21   *Vayikra* 26:16.

through to Hakadosh Baruch Hu through the medium of *avodah zarah*. In their minds they did not consider themselves as having converted to another religion.

We do not know the actual percentage of people who worshipped idols, but we know that it was a widespread practice. However, not only the idol worshippers suffered in the *churban*. We saw earlier that even outstanding *tzaddikim* perished during the *churban*, their only fault being that they hadn't rebuked those who, in their minds, would certainly not heed their words.

FRUM IDOL WORSHIPPERS

As strange as it seems to us, it is clear from the *Tanach* that the idol worshippers kept many mitzvos, if not almost all of them. In the book of *Shoftim*, Gidon repeated what his father had said the previous night while reciting *Hallel* at the Pesach Seder. Then Gidon was commanded to slaughter the ox that his father had fattened for seven years to sacrifice to Baal.

Up until the *churban*, the masses were still fulfilling many mitzvos:

- Traveling to the Beis Hamikdash on Yom Tov
- *Tefillah*
- *Korbanos*
- Belief that Hashem would never allow the Beis Hamikdash to be destroyed and that they too would be protected
- Gathering at times of distress to fast in the Beis Hamikdash

Perhaps they weren't ready to admit their faults and did not fast and do *teshuvah* when necessary. Nevertheless, they still considered themselves *frum* Jews. When Yirmiyahu HaNavi rebuked them for breaking Shabbos, he mentioned only the sin of carrying out into the streets of Yerushalayim on Shabbos—not cooking or building. Had there been other issues of *chillul Shabbos*, the *Navi* would not have refrained from mentioning them! They were therefore still—almost completely—*shomrei Shabbos*. Nevertheless, he warned them that if they did not listen to his rebuke and refrain from carrying out in the street, Yerushalayim would be burned with no one to extinguish the fire.

> *It will be if you listen to Me, says Hashem, not to carry burdens in the gates of the city on the day of Shabbos, and to sanctify the day of Shabbos, not to perform any melachah on it, then there will come into the gates of this city kings and rulers who sit on the throne of David riding on chariots and horses, they with their officers, the people of Yehudah and the inhabitants of Yerushalayim. This city shall remain forever. But if you do not listen to me to sanctify the day of Shabbos, and not to carry burdens and enter the gates of Yerushalayim on the day of Shabbos, then I will ignite a fire in its gates, which will consume the homes of Yerushalayim and not be extinguished.*[22]

NOT EVERYONE, NOT EVERYWHERE

The Gemara demonstrates how we see from the *Tanach* that the people transgressed idolatry, adultery, and murder.[23] Although it seems that idolatry was widespread, the Gemara quotes only the verse that demonstrates that an idol had been brought into the *Kodesh HaKodashim*. Perhaps this was the final straw. For adultery, the Gemara brings a verse stating that the women of Tzion dressed seductively to bring attention to themselves. Nothing is mentioned in the verse about actual adultery. As far as spilling blood is concerned, the Gemara quotes only the verse that Menasheh shed blood across Yerushalayim. The Gemara explains this as referring to the fact that he killed his own grandfather, Yeshayah HaNavi, who opposed him. Perhaps he killed others who stood up against him as well.

We see from the above that not everyone worshipped idols, Yerushalayim was not full of houses of ill repute, nor was there a sniper waiting in every house to shoot passersby. These sins certainly existed to some extent, and it was unacceptable to our Creator. Yet, the entire people were held responsible.

---

22 *Yirmiyahu* 17:19–27.
23 *Yoma* 9b.

THE LAST KING BEFORE THE CHURBAN

The last king before the *churban* of the First Beis Hamikdash, Tzidkiyahu HaMelech, was a superlative *tzaddik*. He would have gone down in history as one of our best kings had he not committed three sins:[24]

- When Nevuchadnetzar put him on the throne, he swore to Nevuchadnetzar that he would not rebel against him. Then he had the Sanhedrin annul his vow, which was not allowed and was also a tremendous *chillul Hashem*.
- He did not rebuke the people as he should have. He was in a position of power, and if he would have told them to stop doing improper acts, for which the *nevi'im* were rebuking them, they would have had to listen.
- He did not listen to the instructions of Yirmiyahu HaNavi, who told him that he should surrender and submit to the authority of Nevuchadnetzar. Had he listened, even at the last minute, the nation would have indeed still been enslaved to Bavel, but the slaughter—the *churban* of the Beis Hamikdash—would not have happened, and Yerushalayim would not have been destroyed. But he couldn't bring himself to do it.

Except for these three sins, he was a perfect *tzaddik*—a *baal mussar* and a *talmid chacham*—but he bore the responsibility for the whole *churban* because it was in his hands to prevent it. Yirmiyahu HaNavi pleaded with him: "I beg of you, go out to Nevuchadnetzar and surrender. The city won't be burned, the Beis Hamikdash won't be destroyed, there won't be a slaughter, and the people will not need to go into exile. If you do not, then you bear responsibility for the entire *churban*." What was his punishment? He saw his ten sons slaughtered before his eyes. Then he was blinded by Nevuchadnetzar's men and was imprisoned in Nevuchadnetzar's very unpleasant jail until he died.

---

24   *Divrei Hayamim II* 36:11–14.

WARNING AFTER WARNING

Throughout the years, the *nevi'im* warned the Jews time and time again. The verse says: "I sent you My servants, the *nevi'im*, sending them bright and early in the morning." There were three main prophets in Yerushalayim then. Yirmiyahu gave his prophecies in the marketplace, Tzefaniah in the shul, and Chuldah told her prophecies to the women. In the end, everything that the *nevi'im* foretold came upon them. For this we mourn every Tishah B'Av.

PURIM AND THE DECREE OF HAMAN

When we observe the holiday of Purim, we are actually celebrating a threatened holocaust that never took place. Haman had decreed that every last Jew would be killed and had royal backing to carry it out. "Mordechai knew all that had happened."[25] *Rashi* explains this to mean that he knew what happened in heaven. Eliyahu HaNavi came to Mordechai and told him that the decree of Haman was made not only on earth but was actually sanctioned in heaven as well.

What did the decree come for? Why was there a threat of annihilation on the Jewish People?

> The talmidim asked Rabbi Shimon ben Yochai, "Why were the [enemies of the] Jewish People guilty of being destroyed in that generation?" He said to them, "Say [the reason] why yourselves." They said, "Because they had derived pleasure from the feast of that rasha [Achashveirosh]." [He responded,] "If so, only those in Shushan should be killed, those in the rest of the world should not be killed." They said to him, "You say [the reason] why." He said, "Because they had bowed to the statue [of Nevuchadnetzar]."[26]

This historical incident is a major lesson in *hashkafah*. Undoubtedly, the people who went to the feast felt they had a valid excuse because Achashveirosh would surely have been angry if all the Jews had refused

---

25 Esther 4:1.
26 Megillah 12a.

to accept his invitation. Nevertheless, it was wrong for them to go to the party. Mordechai, the head of Sanhedrin, had warned them not to go and that the purpose of the party was to cause them to sin, but they did not listen.[27] Eighteen thousand five hundred Jews went to Achashveirosh's party in Shushan. There is no doubt that it was a sin to attend. The atmosphere at the party was highly indecent. Furthermore, the *talmidim* of Rabbi Shimon ben Yochai did not say that the decree came about because of the sin of attending the party or participating in the indecent activities there, but because "they *took pleasure* from the feast of Achashveirosh." The people thoroughly enjoyed themselves. But how is it reasonable that such a misdeed, even if severe, would earn them a decree of annihilation? Moreover, why did the *talmidim* originally think that the Jews' enjoyment of the feast was the reason for the decree, if it was only the Jews of Shushan who attended?

Rabbi Shimon ben Yochai added to their answer. There was another *aveirah* that had been transgressed by the entire people, which preceded their indulgence at Achashveirosh's feast. Many decades before, when the Jewish People were under the rule of Bavel, Nevuchadnetzar had erected a statue.[28] He commanded everyone in his empire to bow to it, and whoever refused would be thrown into a burning furnace. Everyone bowed to it, including all the Jewish People, except for Chananya, Mishael, and Azariah. When they were thrown into the furnace, they were miraculously saved. There is a dispute between the Rishonim if the statue was literally an idol, or it was just made in honor of the king. But even if we grant that it was genuine *avodah zarah*, it is not simple to understand how a decree of annihilation could come for such a sin. *Rambam* tells us that a person who performs a sin upon threat of death is called an *ones*, "one who has been forced,"[29] and he is not held guilty of committing that sin. In the case of idolatry, however, there is a mitzvah to give up one's life rather than to worship, even under duress. Therefore, the Jews certainly did the wrong thing and should have

---

27 *Esther Rabbah* 7:13.
28 *Daniel* 3:6.
29 *Yesodei HaTorah* 5:4.

been held accountable. However, one who does not give his life *is not an idolator* but has merely transgressed the command not to desecrate the name of Hashem. This applies even if it was a real *avodah zarah*. If we were to follow the opinion of *Rabbeinu Tam*[30]—that this was not even a real idol, but only had the trappings and appearance of one—then it becomes extremely difficult to explain how the sin could be held against them to the point of a decree of total destruction! The punishment does not seem to fit the crime!

A possible explanation is that assimilation never begins when people discard their yarmulkas, break Shabbos, or eat *treif*. The process starts long before, when their appreciation for Torah and mitzvos becomes eroded, when their attitudes on life become influenced by society, and their sensitivities are no longer what the Torah wants them to be. When one loses reverence for the *chachamim*, he takes others for role models. Such people do not revel in the things that should make a Jew rejoice and are not put off by the things that should cause disgust and discomfort to a proper, feeling Jew.

If circumstances would require a Jew to enter a bar, where all types of improper behavior are taking place, the barometer of Jewish sensitivity would immediately tell us where that person stands in his Judaism. If he is just hanging onto his Yiddishkeit, going through the motions by rote, but has lost the feelings that a Jew should have, he won't be disgusted by the experience. He may even enjoy it. Perhaps his conscience would prevent him from entering such a place for no reason, but if circumstances necessitate his going in there, he may actually find himself enjoying it. What kind of *chinuch* will such a person give his children? What will he be thinking about when he recites *Shema* or davens? This person is hanging on to his observance by a hair and is headed toward the door marked "exit."

This is precisely what enjoying the party of Achashveirosh signified, with lewd talk and immoral behavior in abundance. How could a Jew attend such a party and not be disgusted? Where were his Jewish feelings

---

30   *Tosafos, Kesubos* 34b.

and sensitivities? And to enjoy himself as well?! The megillah describes at great length the lavishness of the party, seemingly unnecessarily. The subtle message therein is that the glamor was what really pulled them to the party. This was the event of the century, with singers, dancers, and entertainment, inlaid floors, tapestries, and the golden cups. What a party! This was what motivated them. If this was where the heart of Klal Yisrael was, then they were heading rapidly down a very slippery slope. Hashem watches from His place and says, "This is not what I bargained for. I will do something drastic to wake them up. If they respond properly and go back to the way Jews should be, I will save them. If not, they will be destroyed. I demand nothing less than 'a kingdom of nobles and a holy people!'"[31]

So now we see that it wasn't their presence at the party per se; it was what that presence indicated. It showed that they were on the brink of assimilation, that their value system had become so watered down that not only could they go to a party that was the antithesis of what a Jew stands for, but they could actually enjoy it. The *talmidim* of Rabbi Shimon ben Yochai assumed that the Jews in Shushan were no different than all of the Jews in the entire empire. Rabbi Shimon ben Yochai explained to them that this behavior was not necessarily an indication of the behavior of the Jews in other provinces. He said further that an extreme deterioration had begun for all the Jews simultaneously when they had bowed to the statue of Nevuchadnetzar. Even if it was not a sin per se, worshipping an idol—even at gunpoint—was psychologically devastating and caused a tremendous weakening in their adherence to Torah and mitzvos. Now, after all these years, it could even result in enjoying a feast in an immoral environment.

Chazal tell us clearly that the Heavenly purpose in the decree was "to return them to the good [way]." The Jewish People were slipping, but Hashem did not send prophets to rebuke them because they had a track record of not listening to the prophets. Chazal say:

---

31 *Shemos* 19:5–6.

> *The removal of the ring [from Achashveirosh's finger to Haman's finger] was greater for the Jewish People than forty-eight prophets and seven prophetesses, for none of them [had been successful] in getting the Jews to do teshuvah. But the removal of the ring [and the threat of annihilation] caused the entire Jewish People to do teshuvah.*[32]

What would have happened if the Jews had not done *teshuvah*? All of them would have been destroyed. There was a real decree of annihilation on them!

There is a very significant point here which we must not overlook. The Jews in Persia were *frum* Jews. Their value system had become diluted and they were slipping, but they remained *frum* Jews:

- Haman himself testified, "Their laws are different from every people."
- As soon as the decree was declared, what did they do? "Great mourning for the Jews, fasting crying and bemoaning, sackcloth and ashes were put on by the multitude." Only believing Jews fast when they are in distress. Sackcloth and ashes are placed on one's skin to make them uncomfortable and arouse them to *teshuvah*. Who does such things? Irreligious Jews? Surely not! They went to shul, and they cried before Hashem to annul the decree. The megillah sums up the story of Purim by describing it as "the story of the fasts and their outcry."[33] This is what averted the terrible decree. The people ran to shul, said *Tehillim*, and davened day and night.
- Chazal do not tell us that there was idolatry, adultery, or murder among them. There was no Shabbos desecration, no eating *treif* food, or any other sins that would define them as nonobservant.
- After the decree was declared, they did *teshuvah* and were saved. Chazal say that after their salvation, they actually accepted the Torah a second time—a thousand years after the Torah was first

---

32 *Megillah* 14a.
33 *Esther* 9:32.

given at Har Sinai.³⁴ Now they reaffirmed their commitment to Torah in a way that pleased Hashem.

These were *frum* Jews who had merely been slipping. Therefore, a holocaust was threatened—not so much for what they had done, but rather to divert them from where they were headed. The difference was that this holocaust was ultimately not carried out.

THE SECOND BEIS HAMIKDASH

The era of the Second Beis Hamikdash was full of turbulence for most of the four hundred and twenty years during which it stood. In spite of this, it was a time of tremendous Torah activity. The *Anshei Knesses Hagedolah* formulated the earliest version of the Mishnah, and the Tanna'im were busy clarifying the entire *Torah She'baal Peh*. The Gemara tells us that the Jewish People were busy learning Torah and performing deeds of *gemilus chasadim*.³⁵ They were *frum* Jews, to say the least. Their sin was *sinas chinam*, "causeless hatred," involving politicking and in-fighting between groups, especially at the end of the era where one group perpetrated violence against another. There were so many murders taking place that the Sanhedrin stopped judging murder cases for forty years before the destruction of the Beis Hamikdash.³⁶

But the *churban* encompassed everyone, not only the violent and not only the ones who were the cause of the churban to come. This was the generation—an entire generation—that received the full dose of the *Tochachah* in the book of *Devarim*.

BEITAR

The *churban* of Beitar is one of the five things that we commemorate on Tishah B'Av.³⁷ As already cited, a little over fifty years after the *churban Beis Hamikdash*, the Romans had made life impossible for the Jews in Eretz Yisrael. There was a man named Shimon bar Koziva (whom we call Bar Kochva because some of the *chachamim* considered him to

---

34 *Shabbos* 88a.
35 *Yoma* 9b.
36 *Sanhedrin* 41a.
37 Mishnah, *Taanis* 4:6.

be Mashiach, in fulfillment of the verse that says: "A shooting star has set forth from Yaakov."[38]) Even Rabbi Akiva thought he would be the Mashiach.[39] He was a mighty warrior, and he gathered an army of four hundred thousand Jewish soldiers to drive out the Romans.

At first, they chased the Romans completely out of Eretz Yisrael. Subsequently, the Romans came back, conquering one town at a time, starting from the north until they reached Yerushalayim. Bar Kochva and his men escaped to Beitar. Beitar was a city on top of a hill and was very well fortified. There was a long siege, and in the end, "when the sins became too many," our enemies got into the city and there was a massive slaughter, which the Gemara describes as "a river of blood." Even during the siege, however, the yeshivos continued—the *tinokos shel bais rabban*, the children who learned in cheder, did not stop their learning. Rabban Shimon ben Gamliel later applied to himself the verse that says, "My eye has caused me suffering more than all the other people of my city."[40] He said that when he was a *cheder* child in Beitar, there were four hundred shuls and each one had four hundred children. The children used to say that if the enemy enters the city, they will stab them with their writing tools. "In the end, I am the only one left." If that is how many *cheder yingelach* there were, then one can only estimate how many people there were in Beitar! It was a massive, massive *shechitah*.

The Gemara tells us that the people of Beitar had sinned when they did not mourn for the destruction of Yerushalayim. There was a certain feud and rivalry between the two cities, and they had felt mistreated by the people of Yerushalayim. Hence, they were not unhappy when it was destroyed, but they erred, as they should have mourned despite their grudge.

The bottom line of all these tragedies is as follows: If we sin, Hakadosh Baruch Hu patiently waits for us. As Chazal say, "His anger is long in coming, [but eventually] He collects what is His."[41] Although Hashem

---

38   *Bamidbar* 24:17.
39   *Eichah Rabbah* 2:4.
40   *Gittin* 58a; *Eichah Rabbah* 2:4.
41   *Bereishis Rabbah* 67:4.

does not show His anger quickly, in the end, He inevitably collects His dues. A deal is a deal and a contract is a contract; it was all foretold from the beginning. Before each and every major tragedy in history, there was a tremendous decline for many years. When there were prophets, the prophets came day after day to warn the people, just as the bank sends the notice warning of a foreclosure. When there were no prophets, Hakadosh Baruch Hu sent messages in ways that spoke loud and clear, had the Jewish People been open to hearing them.

In all of these instances, we do not hear the Jews asking, "Where was Hashem?"

THE EXPULSION FROM SPAIN

Although there had been a golden era in Spain for a few centuries, during the hundred years before the expulsion, the Jews were attacked again and again. Pogroms were perpetrated in cities throughout Spain. The Church, with the approval of the king and queen, instituted the Spanish Inquisition, which was mainly to ascertain that the conversos did not retain any Jewish practices. Anyone caught doing so was tortured and burned at the stake.

Jews who had already been influenced by the study of philosophy and the easy, pleasant lifestyle in Spain were considerably weakened in their faith, and they fell easy prey to Christian pressure. A very large number succumbed.[42] Among the masses of Jews who converted to Christianity in Spain, many had the intention to continue observing Judaism in secret, in spite of the danger.

Finally, King Ferdinand and Queen Isabella decreed, upon the advice of Torquemada, the head of the Spanish Inquisition, that any Jew who had not yet converted to Christianity by August 1, 1492, would have to either leave Spain or face death. On that day, which corresponded to

---

42   This is one of the few examples in history where mass numbers of Jews were not willing to be martyred to maintain their faith. This was a striking exception to the general pattern of our history, where Jews almost never succumbed to forced conversion. The only other distinct time when such an occurrence took place, though not under threat of death, was after the Reform movement started in Germany. However, even in Spain there were many Jews who refused to give in.

Tishah B'Av, three hundred thousand Jews left their homes and possessions. Most went by rented boats, and many never made it to their destinations. Some of them were thrown overboard by the captains, and many didn't know where they were going or who would take them in. Holland and Turkey did indeed take them in, but many other places did not.

Some Jews went by land to nearby Portugal. Not long after, there was a royal marriage between Spain and Portugal, and the Portuguese king instituted the Inquisition in Portugal. They took tens of thousands of Jewish children by force to the baptismal front.

Among those who were forced into exile and suffered untold horrors were many *talmidei chachamim* and *tzaddikim*. The *Abarbanel*, who had been the finance minister in Spain, was given the privilege of staying, but he refused and went into voluntary exile with his people.

1648-1649

In 1648 and 1649 (the Hebrew years of 5408 and 5409), the Cossacks in the Ukraine staged an uprising against the Polish, who were the landowners of estates in the Ukraine. Many Jews were managers for the nobles, so the Cossacks had a grudge against them. They didn't need much of an excuse to hate Jews because they were fanatic Christians, and the church at the time preached Jew-hatred constantly. Thus, the populace already had it in for the Jews. As the Cossacks marched through Poland, they murdered approximately one-third of the Jewish population. They displayed cruelty and brutality in a manner only equaled by the later behavior of the Nazis in the Holocaust. Of course, they lacked the technology to carry out their slaughter rapidly. They had to do it all by hand with their swords. They showed no mercy to men, women—even those who were pregnant—and children. They were brutal and vicious beyond any imagination.

The Jews in Poland at that time were all *shomrei Torah u'mitzvos*. There was no Reform or Conservative, and there were no secular Jews. The *Gedolim* of the time were hard-pressed to offer some explanation for this tragedy. It is popularly accepted that the *Tosfos Yom Tov* asked a *sh'eilah* from Heaven in a dream and was told that the tragedies came about because of the sin of speaking in shul.

While speaking in shul is a serious *aveirah* because it is disrespectful to a *makom kadosh* and reflects an emotional disconnect between the person and his Creator, these were communities that were *shomrei Torah u'mitzvos* in every sense of the word! Nevertheless, the *middas ha'din* caught up with them and dealt them a very harsh blow. There were great *tzaddikim* among them, as well as children and babies who perished during the massive slaughter that spread through all the towns of Eastern Poland.

These calamities cited are only a sampling of all we have been through. This has been the pattern of every tragedy that ever befell our people, and this is how we have to understand history and the tragedies that have been recorded in our *sefarim*. When we kept the contract, things were better. When we broke it, things turned worse. Does the Heavenly response happen immediately? No! How long does Hakadosh Baruch Hu wait? Sometimes longer, sometimes shorter, all according to calculations known only to Him. Hakadosh Baruch Hu was upset with the Jewish People from when Shlomo HaMelech married the daughter of Pharaoh, down to the destruction of the first Beis Hamikdash—a period of over four hundred years. There was "a suppressed dislike" that entire time. Hakadosh Baruch said, "I'm waiting, I'm waiting." He still treated them with favor. But as they deteriorated, Hashem sent His *nevi'im*, He warned them again and again down to the last minute, and finally Hashem could no longer withhold retribution. This is the way we understand our history.

Throughout our history, the complaint of "Where was Hashem?" was almost never heard. The Jewish People always understood that it was they themselves who were at fault, and they accepted the judgment. They searched within themselves for the sins that might have brought the calamity and said *viduy* with a bent head: "You, Hashem, are correct—and we are shame-faced."[43]

We have shown thus far that the common denominator of all these tragedies that have struck the Jewish People in the past was that the

---

43   Daniel 9:7.

masses had sinned in some way and incurred an evil decree. Through this collective and communal punishment, many *tzaddikim*—who certainly would have been considered by us as unworthy of such a punishment—also suffered. This world is just a temporary corridor; it is a train ride, and for some it is bumpy. When we reach our destination, Hakadosh Baruch Hu will square all accounts in *Olam Haba* to the point where those who suffered will say, "It was a bargain, and I'm happy I went through it."

Nothing that we have written here will alter the realities of life:

- Sickness and poverty remain painful and distressing.
- Old age is very difficult for most.
- Death is inevitable for all.

However, it makes a big difference to a person when he knows that his suffering is not for naught. The true *maamin* remains staunch in his belief that everything that happens comes from Hashem and is ultimately for the good. We will seldom, if ever, fully understand—even when we see glimmers of reward for some *maaminim*.

Summing Up

Reviewing our long and turbulent history teaches us what the Creator expects from us and how He eventually responds when we fall short of His expectations. The pattern seems consistent throughout. As stated earlier, there have been no surprises—for everything that has befallen us was foretold.

We have endeavored to show how limited human understanding really is, especially compared to that of the Creator. Everything that happens is with an exact *cheshbon*, even when we have no clue as to why. No one gets cheated and all accounts are settled fairly, whether in this world or the next. The purpose of this life is not for this world, but rather for the next. All that Hakadosh Baruch Hu does is for the good, even when it doesn't seem good to us. When we internalize these lessons, we can more easily accept the difficulties that come our way.

CHAPTER TWENTY

The Churban of European Jewry

It would be senseless, in a book such as this, to omit any discussion of the Holocaust. After all, we've written about *yissurim* that befall an individual, and *yissurim* that come upon a *tzibbur*. How can we not address the overwhelming tragedy that came upon our people a mere eighty years ago? Perhaps it is reasonable to say that the greatest tragedy in all of history for the Jewish People, at least in terms of numbers and the degree of suffering, was the Holocaust.

There are people who sit in judgment of Hakadosh Baruch Hu, the *kofrim* who scoff at us and say, "Where was G-d? Where was He during the Holocaust? How could He let it happen?" Someone who thinks that the arbiter of fairness is the human mind is destined to be sorely disappointed when he finally confronts His Creator, because no one ever wins a debate with Hakadosh Baruch Hu. Indeed, everything that happens in this world is done only with the infinite *seichel* of the One Above. *Maaminim* never sit in judgment of Hakadosh Baruch Hu. We don't expect what He does to conform with the way we would like it, or with what we think is fair. We know that He knows better. Our intention is merely to see from the Torah how it is that Hakadosh Baruch Hu conducts His affairs in this world. As far as "why" is concerned, what we can understand we want to understand, and what we don't understand we accept without comprehending.

This, however, is a very sensitive issue. Not only are there still survivors among us, but many of their children and grandchildren have all been greatly affected by this horrendous calamity.

To the best of my knowledge, there are only two prevalent approaches to explain what happened during the destruction of European Jewry. Some say that we are at a total loss to explain it, except to say that it is "one of Hashem's secret mysteries." We accept it with total faith in Him. Among the proponents of this response are many great *talmidei chachamim*, *roshei yeshiva*, and Chassidishe Rebbes. These great people have written and spoken publicly about the futility of trying to explain the Holocaust. To their thinking, the idea that the sins of that generation were the cause of the *churban* is an insult to the six million. We have no right to point fingers, and to do so is incongruous with the enormity of what befell them. The six million died *al kiddush Hashem* and are *kedoshim*. We need to remember them, mourn for them, and point out the many times that they were *moser nefesh* to maintain their faith and keep mitzvos according to their ability and circumstances. We are not prophets and cannot know why Hashem would bring such a punishment. When people ask, "Where was G-d and how could He let this happen?" all we can respond is that we don't know, but we have confidence in His judgment.

In stark contrast, there are those who say that it seems clear that the Holocaust was a response to the great and unprecedented defection from Yiddishkeit that took place both in Western and Eastern Europe in the decades leading up to the *churban*. Among the most outspoken of these was Rav Avigdor Miller, in his books and in his recorded *shiurim*. Most recently, a manuscript was found in his drawer and published under the title *A Divine Madness*. In that book he outlined what was, in his opinion, the terrible decline in Yiddishkeit and the *middah k'neged middah* punishment for it. The widespread impression is that Rav Miller stood alone in his position. However, many other *gedolim* did maintain, in no uncertain terms, precisely the same position.

Due to the sensitivity of this issue, I have not recorded the words of those who concurred with Rav Miller here in this volume. For those who would like to pursue the issue and see those quotations, they can simply email me at dsapirman@gmail.com, and I will reply with a PDF.

The author of this book is all too aware of his own insignificance and that he has no right to an opinion on such a subject. Not only because I am unworthy but also because I was never personally affected by the Holocaust. My family has been in America since 1912. As many have rightly said, "Someone who didn't experience this horror has no right to an opinion."

WE BELIEVE WITH PERFECT FAITH

As has been stated numerous times, the purpose of this book is to impart the idea that the Ribbono Shel Olam knows what He is doing, no matter how much or how little we understand the reasoning behind His works. Since we view things only with this-worldly eyes, we act as if this world is all that there is. But the reality is that this life is not the end but merely the beginning. *Olam Hazeh* is merely a fleeting moment compared to the eternity of *Olam Haba*. We may not understand the suffering of an individual who, to our minds, is not deserving of *yissurim*. Nevertheless, we need to accept that it must be so, for Hashem has so decreed. In precisely the same manner must we accept the Creator's judgment on the six million, even if we cannot fathom why they were made to undergo such horrors. Absence of knowing the reason does not detract from our trust in the Almighty.

This being the case, whether we can or cannot explain any reason for this most horrible *churban*, we must still keep reminding ourselves that this world is temporary, *Olam Haba* is forever, and the Ribbono Shel Olam knows what He is doing, even when what happens defies understanding on our part.

Summing Up

The wounds of this most recent horror are too fresh and too enormous for someone such as myself to undertake an explanation of it. We fall back on our three-thousand-year-old *emunah* in the *Borei Olam* that He knows better and that all will be clear someday.

CHAPTER
TWENTY-ONE

Why the Jews?

The Jewish People's history is unlike that of any other nation. Certainly, it is true that nations other than the Jews have been persecuted, attacked, and even murdered—indeed, many times. In that respect the Jewish People are not unique. What is so different about our past is that the occurrences that plague others *occasionally* have been happening to us *consistently* down through the ages. We have been despised, vilified, persecuted, and banished—almost consistently—for close to two thousand years. (That is in addition to the stormy fifteen hundred years prior to our last exile.) Hundreds of thousands have given their lives rather than be forced into accepting a false faith. Wherever Jews have been dispersed around the globe, even after they had some peaceful periods, eventually the host nation turned on them with a fury. After the golden era in Spain, there was a hundred-year period of constant persecutions and murder. Somehow, in the eyes of the world, we always seem to be the bad guys, the convenient scapegoat. If the question of "why the Jews?" is bothersome to you, you are definitely in good company. Are we the worst people in the world? Why do we suffer more than the other nations, whose history is considerably more tranquil than ours? Have we done such terrible things that we deserve to undergo such trauma time and time again? It begs an explanation, especially in a book where we endeavor to make the Divine providence a little more understandable. If, in this book, we address the sufferings of the individual, or the sufferings of the entire people in one particular historical period, isn't it incumbent upon us to address the almost constant pattern of travails that our people have had to bear from anti-Semitism?

THERE HAVE BEEN NO SURPRISES

While we may wonder *why* it must be so—that our people suffer so much in *galus*—it should nevertheless not come to us as a surprise. All of our history was foretold right in the *Chumash*, long before it happened. The total picture of our two-thousand-year exile is forecast in five short verses in the Torah.

> *You will remain small in population, instead of what you were, like the stars of the heavens for many. Because you didn't listen to the voice of Hashem, your G-d.*

The Jewish People will never become very populous in *galus*. Mathematically, they should have multiplied to about a billion over the two thousand years of our exile, but we were told that we would remain small in number, and so we have.

> *And it will be, that just as Hashem rejoiced over you to do good to you and to increase you, so shall He* **cause others to rejoice** *over you to destroy you and to wipe you out.*

In this verse is the prediction of anti-Semitism, with which our enemies rejoice in vilifying and persecuting us without stopping. Their accusations are all baseless, but they persist nevertheless.

> *And Hashem will scatter you from one end of the earth to the other end of the earth.*

The dispersion of our people around the globe is part and parcel of the exile. There are Jewish communities from South Africa to Australia, from South America to Europe, and almost anywhere else in the globe—and so it has been since the beginning of our *galus*.

> *And there you will serve other gods that you and your forefathers never knew [before],* **wood and stone.**

"Serve" here means be under their rule. The Vilna Gaon says that wood is the wooden cross of Christianity, and stone is the symbol of Islam (the stone at Mecca). These are the two nations that have caused us the most hardships. All this was foreseen in advance.

*And among those nations **you shall not be at ease**.*

This first half of this verse predicts the persecutions and discrimination that we have undergone in just about every country where Jews have resided.[1]

Nor will there be a resting place for the sole of your foot.

No country will be a permanent residence for you. Jews were banished from almost every country in which they have resided. That includes (among many others) from England for three hundred years, and from Spain after living there for hundreds of years. Between the two world wars, after a significant Jewish presence in Poland for a thousand years, they said, "Jews, go home!"

*And Hashem will give you **there** a trembling heart, despair, and anguish.*

The *galus* Jew will be timid and meek, seldom taking the measures to protect himself. (Most often, their circumstances made it impossible to do so. That, too, is part of the *galus*.) The Jews were not that way before they were exiled by the Romans, and the Israelis are certainly not timid and meek. But in the diaspora that is how they will be.

Seemingly, then, there ought not to have been any surprises. But the question *why* still needs to be addressed.

THE ETERNAL NATION

We cannot compare the other nations of the world to the Jewish nation. Only the Jewish People have a promise from Hashem that they

---

1   Most of the readers are living in countries that are the exception to the historical pattern of our exile. We hope and pray that it will continue to be so, but we have no guarantee.

will always survive crises and continue to exist. Their Torah will survive with them forever as well. Other nations have no such guarantee.

The following are a few statements from *Tanach* that express this idea.

Eternal Covenant

> *And even with all this [terrible retribution], while they are still in the land of their enemies, I will not loathe them or reject them, to nullify My covenant with them, for I am Hashem, their G-d.*[2]

In this verse, Hashem promised us that He will never reject us for our sins, for His covenant with us is eternal.

More Eternal Than the Mountains

Yeshayah HaNavi said:

> *For this is to Me like the waters of Noach, about which I swore that the waters of Noach would not pass over on the earth again. So, too, have I sworn to never be [excessively] angry at you or to [excessively] rebuke you. For [even if] the mountains will be removed and the hills will depart, My kindness with you will not be removed, and My covenant of peace will not depart, said Hashem, Who has mercy on you.*[3]

The Jewish People will continue to exist as long as there are mountains and hills, and even longer. Hashem swore so.

More Eternal Than the Heavenly Bodies

> *So said Hashem, who gives the sun for the light of day, the regulations of the moon and the stars for the light of night, Who stirs up the sea and [makes] its waves roar, the Lord of Hosts is His name. If these regulations shall be removed before Me,*

---

2 *Vayikra* 26:44.
3 *Yeshayah* 54:9.

says Hashem, [then] also the children of Yisrael will cease to be a nation before me all the days.[4]

The Jewish People have been promised that they will always exist as Hashem's special nation. No matter how many sins they have committed, they will never be rejected. As long as there is a sun and a moon, mountains and hills, there will always be Am Yisrael.

THE GREAT DIFFERENCE BETWEEN YISRAEL AND THE NATIONS

When other nations revolt against Hashem, their Creator is not in a hurry to punish them. The Gemara tells us that "HaKadosh Baruch Hu does not bring retribution on a nation until their measure [of sins] is filled." When their sins "fill up their measure," He brings on them whatever sufferings His wisdom decrees. If He feels they deserve it, He simply eliminates them from the world. That is precisely what happened to the empires that oppressed us in the past. They were the mightiest for a while, and then when their time came, they either disappeared or paled into insignificance. Nevuchadnetzar's world empire lasted a mere seventy years. Then the Babylonians were conquered by the Persians, never to lift their heads as a world power again. Spain was once a mighty world power. Not long after they expelled our people from Spain, the English armada defeated them, and Spain has not been a major player on the world scene for the last five hundred years.

Not so the Jewish People. Hashem will never allow their measure of sins to become full because they have a promise from Hashem that they will be an eternal nation. If their measure of sins would be allowed to fill up, then they, too, would have to be destroyed, which Hashem will never permit. The *nevi'im*, in many more places than those already quoted, have told us repeatedly that no matter how much travail we will suffer, there will never be a complete destruction of our people. Therefore, instead of destroying us when our sins accumulate, He takes payments regularly through the hard times that we endure. We learn this concept

---

4 Yirmiyahu 31:34.

in the Gemara. The Christian heretics posed a valid question to Rabbi Abahu:[5] "The verse states: 'Only you I love from all the families of the earth. Therefore, I visit all your sins upon you.'[6] If someone is in a rage, does he vent it on his beloved friend?" Why would Hashem punish all the sins of specifically the Jewish People if they are His beloved?

Rabbi Abahu responded, "This can be explained with an allegory. If two people each owe someone a debt, one is his friend and one is his enemy, he lets his friend pay the debt out slowly, but makes his enemy pay it up all at once."

What Rabbi Abahu said here is precisely the concept we have just written. From other nations He takes payment in one shot, whereas from the Jewish People, He takes payment by giving them *yissurim* bit by bit so that they are never allowed to fill up their measure and perish.

Rambam also expresses this idea.[7] When we explain to a newly converted *ger* why the Jewish People suffer so much, we tell him that "HaKadosh Baruch Hu does not bring on them excessive retribution in order that they should not perish. Rather, all the other nations will perish, but they will remain."

TRANQUILITY IS NOT CONDUCIVE TO ATTAINING OLAM HABA

The basic theme of this book is that this world is merely a preparation for *Olam Haba*. All that happens here is intertwined with each individual's account there. *Rambam* draws on this concept to explain the *tzaros* we undergo. When a gentile converts, we must inform him of the punishments for sins, to give him the opportunity to back out if he wants to. However, we also must inform him of the great reward that awaits the righteous of Yisrael.

> *Just as we inform him of the punishments for aveiros, we must also inform him of the reward for mitzvos. We tell him that by doing these mitzvos, he will merit the life of Olam Haba.*

---

5   Avodah Zarah 4a.
6   Amos 3:2.
7   Rambam, Issurei Biah 14:5.

> There is no one who is a true complete tzaddik but the person who is wise and keeps these mitzvos and knows them well. And we say to him, "Know that the afterlife is hidden away only for the righteous, that is Yisrael. **That which you see that the Jewish People are in distress in this world is a hidden favor for them.** They are not able to receive a multitude of good in this world, as do the other nations, for perhaps their heart will become arrogant, they will stray and lose the reward of Olam Haba." As it says in a verse:[8] "Yeshurun [the Jewish People] became fat and kicked [rebelled]."[9]

FORECLOSURE

There is another reason that the Jewish People have been singled out for hard times. Imagine that your next-door neighbors are just the sweetest people ever. Such nice people! The father would give you the shirt off his back. If you had a flat tire, he'd be under your car fixing it for you. The mother is always baking for a neighbor who had a baby or for someone who's sick. They're just wonderful, nice people. To your shock, one day, the sheriff shows up at their house, chases them out, and puts a padlock on their door. They're out on the street. You say to yourself, "How is it possible that this could happen to such a nice family?" But the answer is all too obvious. They simply didn't pay the mortgage. They had taken out a mortgage, but they didn't make the payments. The bank sent them a statement saying that they're overdue one payment, then two payments. Finally, after a long time, they sent them a final notice that their house would have to be foreclosed if they didn't pay by a certain date. The deadline passed, and the bank foreclosed on them. Now they find themselves out on the street.

That's exactly what Hakadosh Baruch Hu did with us. We entered into a contract. It says in the contract: "You must be to Me a nation of nobles and a holy people."[10] Hashem promised us every benefit we can imagine

---

8   *Devarim* 32:15.
9   *Rambam, Issurei Biah* 14:3–4.
10 *Shemos* 19:6.

if we keep our end of the deal. But what He expects in return is "a nation of nobles and a holy people." If you listen, everything will be good for you, in countless ways. But if you don't, there will be serious consequences. You're going to be on the bottom. That's why we can't ask, "Why did these things happen to the Jewish People but not to anyone else? Are we worse than all the others?"

ARE WE THE WORST?

No, we're not the worst. In many ways, we're actually much better than others. Jewish People still do more for Hakadosh Baruch Hu and sacrifice more than anyone else! But the other nations never made a contract with Hakadosh Baruch Hu. We did, and we reneged on our agreement. Hakadosh Baruch Hu said, I sent you a notice, you're overdue one payment, then two payments, there's going to be a foreclosure. He waited two hundred and fifty years for the ten tribes, and much longer for the land of Yehudah: "He sent His servants the *nevi'im* to them, but they made fun of them."[11] Hakadosh Baruch Hu gave them a chance down to the last minute, but they refused. They thought they knew better and could get away with it. But we signed a contract and reneged, and Hashem finally collected.

Imagine a trucking company that entered into a million-dollar contract to transport merchandise from the East Coast to the West Coast, but the company didn't bother doing the shipping. They missed the stipulated deadline, so now they are being taken to court to be heavily penalized. It's all so very simple. If you abide by the contract, you get what you were promised. If you break the contract, you're in trouble. No other trucking company can expect to get the million in salary, and no other company can be taken to court. They never signed a contract. But Klal Yisrael did indeed sign a contract and then broke it. True, we weren't—and aren't—cannibals or mafia gangsters, but we're also far from what was agreed upon in the deal. Hashem says, "I didn't take the Jewish People to be my chosen nation just so they should be 'nice guys.' No! 'A nation of nobles and a holy people!' That was the agreement.

---

11   *Divrei Hayamin II* 36:15.

I won't settle for less." I sent them one notice (a *navi*), a second notice, and numerous subsequent notices, one after another. I brought mini-*churban* warnings on them so they should realize that I was about to foreclose, but they went about their merry sinful ways, confidently ignoring my warnings. Finally, I foreclosed.

FOILING THE MASTER PLAN OF CREATION

It's actually much more than just an issue of a broken agreement. Chazal have taught us that Hakadosh Baruch Hu created the world on a condition. In the story of creation, it says *a* second day, *a* third day, etc. Concerning the sixth day it says: "*The* sixth day."[12] The world would have to wait for *the sixth day* of Sivan. If B'nei Yisrael will accept the Torah, the world will remain. However, if Klal Yisrael will not accept the Torah, Hakadosh Baruch Hu will bring the world back to *tohu va'vohu* (nothingness).

The first word in the Torah, "*Bereishis*,"[13] is grammatically difficult, because it really means, "in the beginning *of.*" *Rashi* says in one explanation that the word *Bereishis* means "for the sake of the Jewish People and the Torah, which are both nicknamed '*reishis.*' The Torah is "the first of Hashem's way,"[14] and the Jewish People are "the first of Hashem's crop."[15] For the sake of these two "firsts," Hashem created heaven and earth. If the Jewish People don't accept the Torah, the world has no reason to exist. When Jews transgress the Torah, Hashem says, "Not only do your personal sins harm yourself, but you're actually destroying My world! You are foiling My plan in creating the world! I made the world for Klal Yisrael to be what Klal Yisrael has to be. And if you don't do what you were created for, then the world has no purpose to exist!" So, you understand, it's like someone whose finger is holding back the water in the dike in Holland. All he did was pull his finger out, so what's the big deal? But he flooded the entire country!

---

12   *Bereishis* 1:31.
13   *Bereishis* 1:1.
14   *Mishlei* 8:22.
15   *Yirmiyahu* 2:3.

SOMEDAY WE'LL UNDERSTAND AND APPRECIATE

The travails of our people can be compared to a person who has a terminal illness, *Rachmana litzlan*. There is no cure for this illness except a certain therapy, which is the most painful, excruciating therapy imaginable. The person said, "I refuse to go through the treatment. I'd rather die. Forget it! There's no way I'm going to do it." His brother, who desperately wanted him to live, took him, tied him up, and brought him to that therapist against his will. The therapist connected all the necessary needles and wires. The therapy took three hours, and the patient was screaming bloody murder. At the end of the three hours, the therapist took off the wires, removed the needles, and said, "Okay, now you're cured. It's all over, and you can go home and lead a normal life." Is the patient grateful to his brother or angry at him?

Now that it's over and done with, of course he's grateful. When Hakadosh Baruch Hu brings upon us whatever He brings in this temporary life, we have to know that, somehow, it's a cure so that we can live a *chayei netzach*, an eternal life. There, in the world of truth, the recipient will be thanking Hashem profusely for his suffering because the recompense was so enormous. It will truly have been worth going through the *yissurim*.

PERSPECTIVE ON THE PANDEMIC

At the time that the bulk of this book was written, not I nor anyone else could have dreamed that the world would soon be turned upside down. With much of the world in lockdown, a suffering economy, high numbers of people who are sick, and no real end in sight, we don't know what the next moment will bring. Perhaps by the time this book appears on the shelves, it will all be just a memory, but perhaps not.

Truthfully, however, the tools provided in this book are the same for this situation as for all the other situations we have discussed. One thing we must remember. When a punishment comes on the whole world, the main address is Klal Yisrael. They are the main actors on the stage of life. Others are merely the supporting cast. The Ribbono Shel Olam knows precisely what He is doing, whether we comprehend it or not. All the possible reasons for *yissurim* presented in this book apply equally to this distress just as for all the other difficulties we encounter. Perhaps it is to arouse us to *teshuvah*, atonement. Maybe the *chashuve* people who passed away were taken as a *korban* for the generation. We certainly don't know. If we had a *navi*, he could tell us—but we do not.

If, as indeed we should assume, our Creator is showing us His disfavor with some of our behaviors, we need to carefully scrutinize our actions to pinpoint our faults. It won't be terribly difficult because anyone with a little common sense can easily recognize the many shortcomings in our generation that are long in need of correction: compromised *tefillah*, lack of honesty in business, obsession with technology, laxity in matters of *kedushah*, *bitul Torah*, *lashon hara*, and sadly many more. When we are placed in a situation where it is clear that Hashem is not happy with us, we are required to seek out whatever needs fixing and get busy making repairs.

I HAD TO DO IT ALL

Here is a final insight before we close.[16] The *Rambam* and the *Ibn Ezra* were contemporaries and good friends. One time the *Ibn Ezra* came to visit the *Rambam*. The *Rambam* was a busy physician and had many other communal involvements. It wasn't surprising, therefore, that he said to the *Ibn Ezra*, "My dear friend, I don't have time for you this minute. Would you mind waiting for me in here?" He opened up a gate, and the *Ibn Ezra* walked in. He heard that the gate was being locked from the outside behind him. When the *Ibn Ezra* looked around, he realized, to his amazement, that he had been locked in a corral of goats. He couldn't believe that his friend, the *Rambam*, would do this to him, so he expected that surely the *Rambam* would be back in a moment. There had to be some mistake. More and more time passed, and all the while the *Ibn Ezra* was searching his soul to find what he could have possibly done to make the *Rambam* embarrass him and belittle him by locking him in a corral of goats. After quite a long while passed, he started to

---

16 Although I remember seeing this story, I am not sure that such a meeting between these two great people could have actually historically taken place. The moral of the story, however, is most appropriate in our context.

bawl out of frustration, crying his eyes out. At that moment, the gate opened and the *Rambam* came in. He gave the *Ibn Ezra* a big hug and a kiss. "My precious friend," he said, "please forgive me! You know that I am a doctor, and when I looked into your eyes, I saw that you have a very serious eye ailment that can only be cured by crying copious tears. So I had to lock you in here in order to bring you to such crying."

This is precisely what our Creator will tell us when we have that eventual meeting with Him. "My child, you couldn't understand at the time, but everything I did needed to be done."

When the *geulah* finally comes, we will have considerably greater clarity on why we had to go through this long and bitter *galus*. Just as we find in a verse we quoted earlier: "I will thank You, Hashem, for being wrought with me. [Now] let Your anger turn away, and console me!"[17] At that time, Hakadosh Baruch Hu will say to us, "My children! Everything I did was absolutely necessary! There was no other way."

In Final Summation

Many mysteries still remain. We still cannot fully discern the pattern of the travails that humans go through. Nevertheless, knowing even in a general way that everything in life serves a purpose and is ordained by the Creator can provide a sense of comfort and relief. We know we are in the very best hands. He wants only our good, and our good deeds are never lost and never go unrecorded. No matter what happens to us in this world, we can look forward to our ultimate destination with a most positive attitude, with peace of mind and tranquility. May *Hashem Yisborach* grant that all the readers, and indeed all of Klal Yisrael, be spared from all harm and suffering. But if and when hardship befalls us, the *mesorah* of *emunah* can soften the experience and enable us to carry on with life and our service to Hashem. May we soon merit that day of great rejoicing, when we will greet *Mashiach Tzidkeinu*. Amen.

---

17   *Yeshayah* 12:1.

About the Author

Rabbi Dovid Sapirman is a former *talmid* of the Philadelphia, Ponovezh, and Lakewood yeshivas. During his fifty years in the field of *chinuch*, he has been a *melamed*, *maggid shiur*, *mashgiach ruchani*, and public speaker and has worked extensively in *kiruv rechokim* and *kiruv kerovim*. In 2009, Rabbi Sapirman founded the Ani Maamin Foundation, dedicated to offering *chizuk* in *emunah* to *bnei Torah* of all ages and backgrounds. Since its creation, the foundation has held presentations for over 50,000 people around the world, created three popular CD series on *inyanei emunah*, and published the bestselling *Emunah: A Refresher Course* (Mosaica Press, 2015).

Rabbi Sapirman is the author of *The Unbroken Chain: The Oral Torah System from Sinai* (Mosaica Press, 2019). He lives in Toronto, Canada, with his family and can be contacted at dsapirman@gmail.com.

לעילוי נשמות
רפאל בר יצחק ע"ה
חיה רוזא איבון בת ישעיה ע"ה
מרדכי בן זאב ע"ה

ROBERT HORT AND VICTORIA MASSIAS-HORT

לעילוי נשמת
ישראל יצחק בן מיכאל הכהן ע"ה
רבקה בת משה ניסן ע"ה
חיים אליהו בן בנימן ע"ה

THE BERENBLUT FAMILY

לעילוי נשמת
ר' עקיבא איגר בן חיים יחזקאל ע"ה
בלימא שבע עלקא בת ר' גרשון ע"ה

לעילוי נשמת האשה החשובה
חיה שרה בת ר' אהרן ע"ה

לעילוי נשמת
דבורה בת משה ע"ה

לעילוי נשמת
שרה בת ר' יעקב ע"ה
In memory of Sally Weitz

לעילוי נשמת
יעקב מנחם מנדל בן מאיר ע"ה
חיה בת יחזקאל ע"ה
פנחס בן יואל ע"ה
פייגא דבורה בת ר' שמואל אליהו ע"ה
משה צבי בן אברהם יצחק ע"ה
איתה בת דוב בערל ע"ה
צבי משה דיימן ע"ה
חנה דיימן ע"ה

לעילוי נשמת
ר' ישראל בן נפתלי הנדלסמן ע"ה
עבר שנות השואה ונשאר עובד ד' בתמימות כל ימיו
נדבת בנו ומשפחתו

לעילוי נשמת
פעריל בת ר' יהושע העשיל הכהן ע"ה
ר' זאב בן ר' יהודה ע"ה

לעילוי נשמת
שרה בת יעקב ע"ה
שולמית בת מרדכי ניסן ע"ה
אהרן יעקב בן נחמיה ע"ה

לעילוי נשמת
ר' יצחק מאיר בן ר' לייב ע"ה
יוכבד בת ר' חיים ע"ה

לעילוי נשמת
זאב בן שלמה ע"ה שידלאוו
ליפשא בת ר' משה דוד ע"ה שידלאוו

In honour of our Rav
Rabbi Avraham Bartfeld שליט"א

לעילוי נשמת
נפתלי הרצקא טוביה בן אלתר מרדכי הכהן מנדלבוים ע"ה
ואשתו קיילא פייגא בת אהרן ע"ה

BAIS DOV YOSEF

לעילוי נשמת

סבא שלנו היקר
ישראל בן אשר אפרים הלוי גורודצקי ע"ה
זכה לראות נכדים ונינים שומרי תורה ומצוות

ציפורה בת יצחק Shier ע"ה
אהובה לכל מכיריה

יצחק בן ישראל Shier ע"ה
איש נדיב ואדיב

לעילוי נשמת
ר' אברהם בן שאול ע"ה

לעילוי נשמת
רחל בת מרדכי Zicherman ע"ה
אברהם צבי בן שמואל מנחם Zicherman ע"ה

לעילוי נשמת
ר' אפרים בן ר' נח ע"ה
מאשא לאה בת ר' זאב ע"ה

לעילוי נשמת
מירי בת מזל טוב ע"ה

לעילוי נשמת
שרה אסתר בת ירחמיאל ע"ה

In honor of our wonderful parents
Dr. and Mrs. Mark Nusbaum
Mr. and Mrs. Howard Pomper
In memory of our beloved mother
Edith Nusbaum ע"ה
SUZY AND MARK POMPER AND FAMILY

MOSAICA PRESS
BOOK PUBLISHERS
Elegant, Meaningful & Bold

info@MosaicaPress.com
www.MosaicaPress.com

The Mosaica Press team of acclaimed editors and designers is attracting some of the most compelling thinkers and teachers in the Jewish community today. Our books are available around the world.

HARAV YAACOV HABER
RABBI DORON KORNBLUTH